CULTURES OF THE WORLD

Iraq

Cavendish
Square
New York

Published in 2015 by Cavendish Square Publishing, LLC
243 5th Avenue, Suite 136, New York, NY 10016

Copyright © 2015 by Cavendish Square Publishing, LLC

First Edition

Website: cavendishsq.com

This publication represents the opinions and views of the author based on his or her personal experience, knowledge, and research. The information in this book serves as a general guide only. The author and publisher have used their best efforts in preparing this book and disclaim liability rising directly or indirectly from the use and application of this book.

CPSIA Compliance Information: Batch #WS14CSQ

All websites were available and accurate when this book was sent to press.

Library of Congress Cataloging-in-Publication Data
Hassig, Susan.
 Iraq / Susan Hassiq, Laith Muhmood, Yong Lin.
  pages cm. — (Cultures of the world)
 Includes bibliographical references and index.
 ISBN 978-0-76144-994-2 (hardcover) ISBN 978-0-76147-994-9 (ebook)
 1. Iraq—Juvenile literature. I. El-Hamamsy, Salwa. II. Elias, Josie. III. Title.
 DS70.62.P38 2014
 956.7—dc23
                          2014011780

Writers: Susan Hassig, Laith Muhmood Al Adely—2nd ed., Deborah Nevins—3rd ed.
Editorial Director Third Edition: Dean Miller
Editor Third Edition: Deborah Nevins
Art Director, Third Edition: Jeffrey Talbot
Designer Third Edition: Jessica Nevins
Production Manager: Jennifer Ryder-Talbot
Production Editors: Andrew Coddington and David McNamara
Picture Researcher Third Edition: Jessica Nevins

The photographs in this book are used by permission through the courtesy of: Cover photo by Dean Conger/National Geographic/Getty Images; James Gordon/File:Marsh Arab Girl.jpg/Wikimedia Commons, 1; Aziz1005/File:Babylon city Iraq.jpg/Wikimedia Commons, 3; Jane Sweeney/Lonely Planet Images/Getty Images, 5; Kamira/Shutterstock.com, 6; Red On/Shutterstock.com, 7; Haidar Hamdani/AFP/Getty Images, 8; Eystein Lund Andersen/E+/Getty Images, 10; Tim Bewer/Lonely Planet Images /Getty Images, 11; Jim Gordon/File:Canyon, north Eastern Kurdistan.jpg/Wikimedia Commons, 12; Essam Al-Sudani/AFP/Getty Images, 13; J. Baylor Roberts/National Geographic/Getty Images, 14; Stringer/Anadolu Agency/Getty Images, 15; Essam Al-Sudani/AFP/Getty Images, 16; Hardnfast/File:Ancient ziggurat at Ali Air Base Iraq 2005.jpg/Wikimedia Commons, 17; Boris Roessler/AFP/Getty Images, 18; Wathiq Khuzaie/Getty Images, 19; Ahmad Al-Rubaye/AFP/Getty Images, 20; Jane Sweeney/Lonely Planet Images/Getty Images, 22; DeAgostini/Getty Images, 23; Mario Tama/Getty Images, 25; Howard Sochurek/Time Life Pictures/Getty Images, 28; Selouk Perin/AFP/Getty Images, 29; Jean-Claude Delmas/AFP/Getty Images, 30; Michel Gangne/AFP/Getty Images, 31; Ali Al-Saadi/AFP/Getty Images, 32; Ahmad Al-Rubaye/AFP/Getty Images, 34; Marc152d/Shutterstock.com, 36; Ap Photo/Ina/Ho, 37; U.S. Marine Corps/File:USMarineTankinBaghdad.jpg/Wikimedia Commons, 38; Sgt. 1st Class Johancharles Van Boers/File:M113-ambulance-fallujah.jpg/Wikimedia Commons, 39; Unknown/File:Saddam capture.jpg/Wikimedia Commons, 40; Gilles Bassignac/Gamm Rapho/Getty Images, 41; Olivier Pool/Getty Images, 42; Getty Images, 43; Sadam el-Mehmedy/AFP/Getty Images, 45; Sabah Arar/AFP/Getty Images, 46; © Ap Images/Nabil Al-Jurani, 48; Dr Ajay Kumar Singh/Shutterstock.com, 49; Ahmad Al-Rubaye/AFP/Getty Images, 50; Shwan Mohammed/AFP/Gettyimages, 51; © Ap Images/Alaa Al-Marjani, 52; Sabah Arar/AFP/Getty Images, 53; Georges Merillon/Gamma-Rapho/Getty Images, 54; Philippe Desmazes/AFP/Getty Images, 55; Randy Olson/National Geographic/Getty Images, 56; Aleks49/Shutterstock.com, 57; Marwan Naamani/AFP/Getty Images, 58; Ahodges7/File:Iraq Oil Well Fire.jpg/Wikimedia Commons, 59; Essam Al-Sudani/AFP/Getty Images, 60; Alfred De Montesquiou/Getty Images, 61; Safin Hamed/AFP/Getty Images, 62; Philippe Desmazes/AFP/Getty Images, 63; Mehdi Fedouach/AFP/Getty Images, 64; Chris Hondros/Getty Images, 65; Wathiq Khuzaie/Getty Images, 66; Tekstbureau De Eindredactie /Flickr Vision/Getty Images, 67; Oleg Nikishin/Photonica World/Getty Images, 68; Ahmad Al-Rubaye/AFP/Getty Images, 69; Ali Al-Saadi/AFP/Getty Images, 70; Ahmad Al-Rubaye/AFP/Getty Images, 71; Safin Hamed/AFP/Getty Images, 72; The Washington Post/Getty Images, 75; Ali Al-Saadi/AFP/Getty Images, 77; Staff Sgt. Adelita Mead/File:Iraqi medical students at Basra University College of Medicine (2010).jpg/Wikimedia Commons, 78; fpolat69/Shutterstock.com, 80; Joshua Haviv/Shutterstock.com, 81; Anadolu Agency/Getty Images, 83; Crystalina/File:Quran cover.jpg/Wikimedia Commons, 86; Sadik Gulec/Shutterstock.com, 87; Fedor Selivanov/Shutterstock.com, 88; Stan Honda/AFP/Getty Images, 89; Ryan Rodrick Beiler/Shutterstock.com, 90; Safin Hamed/AFP/Getty Images, 92; federicofoto/Shutterstock.com, 94; Ahmad Al-Rubaye/AFP/Getty Images, 95; pio3/Shutterstock.com, 96; Patricia Hofmeester/Shutterstock.com, 97; Getty Images, 98; Patrick Baz/AFP/Getty Images, 99; Ahmad Al-Rubaye/AFP/Getty Images, 100; Akram Saleh/Getty Images, 101; Jasmine N. Walthall/File:Ruins from a temple in Naffur.jpg/Wikimedia Commons, 102; Arlo K. Abrahamson/File:US Navy 030525-N-5362A-004 U.S. Sailors and Marines attached to Camp Babylon, Iraq, take a guided tour of the ancient ruins of Babylon located near their compound.jpg/Wikimedia Commons, 103; Essam Al-Sudani/AFP/Getty Images, 104; Deagostini/Getty Images, 105; Joe Raedle/The Image Bank/Getty Images, 106; René Bull/File:Sinbad 1.jpg/Wikimedia Commons, 108; Ahmad Al-Rubaye/AFP/Getty Images, 110; Jane Sweeney/The Image Bank/Getty Images, 111; Ali Al-Saadi/AFP/Getty Images, 112; Ali Al-Saadi/AFP/Getty Images, 114; Anadolu Agency/Getty Images, 115; Ali Al-Saadi/AFP/Getty Images, 117; Ahmad Al-Rubaye/AFP/Getty Images, 118; Ali Al-Saadi/AFP/Getty Images, 119; Jane Sweeney/Lonely Planet Images/Getty Images, 122; Ahmad Al-Rubaye/AFP/Getty Images, 123; Ali Al-Saadi/AFP/Getty Images, 126; Sabah Arar/AFP/Getty Images, 127; Northfoto/Shutterstock.com, 128; Tyler Nevins, 132; Tyler Nevins, 133.

Preceding Page:
A Marsh Arab girl stands in front of a traditional reed house in the endangered marshlands of southern Iraq.

Printed in the United States of America

CONTENTS

IRAQ TODAY

IRAQ IS A HARD PLACE. THIS MIDDLE EASTERN COUNTRY HAS BEEN in the news a great deal in recent years, and the news has rarely been good. Over the past thirty years, Iraq has fought three major wars, endured a long, brutal dictatorship, and suffered twelve years of international sanctions. These trade barriers were aimed at punishing the government of the tyrannical president Saddam Hussein. In the end, however, the sanctions simply pushed an already oppressed people to their knees. After the U.S.-led invasion of their country in 2003, many Iraqis rejoiced at the demise of the dictator. But then they had no choice but to tolerate being occupied by a foreign military.

The United States withdrew most of its forces from the country in 2011, but the Iraqi people continue to face ongoing hardship. Iraqis who were once neighbors are suddenly enemies, on opposite sides of a religious sectarian divide. Sunni Muslims, Shia Muslims, Kurds—all these Iraqis have their own vision for the future; all have their particular complaints. A coalition government, Iraq's first attempt at representative democracy, struggles to rule effectively and fairly, but it's a huge task to guide such a battered and beaten nation. Charges of corruption sap the people's

This Mesopotamian relief portrays an Assyrian warrior hunting a lion.

trust. Old injustices still fester. The people grow disillusioned and impatient. Some people resort to terrorism. Violence escalates and the country teeters on the brink of civil war.

Iraq is a special place. With a history going back more than 6,000 years, it is the site of the world's earliest civilization—Mesopotamia. Iraq's heritage as "the cradle of civilization" belongs not only to this one troubled nation, but to the world. In some ways, Iraq is one big archaeological site, a modern world sitting on top of an ancient one. Under this soil, as many as 25,000 cities may lie in ruins, awaiting the light of discovery. Here lies Ur, one of the oldest cities, and possible birthplace of the biblical Abraham. Here lies Babylon, a city of great splendor some 2,500 years ago. Its mythic hanging gardens are listed among the Seven Wonders of the Ancient World.

The growth of Mesopotamia—and of Iraq itself several millennia later—

followed the course of two great rivers, the Tigris and the Euphrates, and the warm, well-watered lands between them. It was here that humans learned to grow their own food. In fact, this was the land of many firsts: the first writing, the first irrigation system, the first legal code. Here is where people invented the wheel, the sail, and concepts of math, time, and astrology. This is where archaeologists discovered the first love song.

With Iraq's natural beauty, rich oil reserves, and extraordinary wealth of history lying beneath its soil, why isn't it one of the happiest places on Earth? Surely the excavation of ancient treasures could establish Iraq as an archaeological research center and fuel a thriving tourist industry.

In fact, the main visitors to some of Iraq's most valuable archaeological sites over the past several decades have been looters. Researchers say that in the past few years, robbers dug the equivalent of 3,700 acres of holes in archaeological sites. A stable and relatively safe Iraq is necessary

A verdant Iraqi garden flourishes in the land described as the "Fertile Crescent."

for research work to resume, and Iraqi scholars are eager to do so. Indeed, after twenty years of waiting, archaeologists from the United States and other countries have recently returned. The Mesopotamian cities of Babylon, Ur, and Nineveh are just partially excavated, with much more to do.

Meanwhile, today's Iraqis struggle to fix the broken country on top of the soil. Under the iron fist of Saddam Hussein, who ruled from 1979 to 2003, Iraqis enjoyed a kind of stability. It was a stability enforced through fear, and purchased at the expense of individual and media freedom, and with the deaths of thousands of people, but it had some benefits. Literacy and education improved tremendously. Western observers applauded the growth of a secular Muslim society in Saddam's Iraq. More than in many other Muslim countries, government was kept separate from the religious sphere, and religious extremism was held at bay. Women were guaranteed equal treatment under the civil Personal Status Law of 1959, which of course

An Iraqi girl holds up a placard supporting the new personal status law that would severely restrict women's rights.

predated the Hussein regime. For women, that law was one of the most progressive in all of the Middle East. Iraq was a pioneer for women's rights among Arab nations.

After the debacle of the first Gulf War, Saddam began to align himself more with the religious sector in Iraq. Observers theorized that Saddam thought by portraying himself as an observant Muslim, he could protect himself and win support. During those years, fundamentalists gained strength, and today, with Saddam gone, they represent a powerful segment of society.

As these conservative clerics gain influence, many Iraqis—and human rights activists around the world—are voicing concern that the hard-earned advances in women's rights will be greatly set back. In 2014 the Iraqi Council of Ministers approved a new personal status code for Shia Muslims which hands family matters—that is, cases of marriage, divorce, inheritance, and custody—back to the Shia religious authorities. If passed by Parliament, the law would legalize polygamy. According to Islamic Sharia law, a man may have up to four wives. It would also require a woman to submit to her husband's will in all matters. Perhaps most upsetting to many observers, the law would allow child marriage; that is, the right of men to marry girls as young as nine years old, and possibly even younger.

With its roots in Sharia law dating back to the eighth century, child marriage is still allowed in some parts of the Islamic world today. If this law passes, it will be a setback for Iraqi girls and women, at least in the view of many people. It would also set up separate laws for Iraqis of different religious affiliations, and require separate courts. That would add to the fracturing of Iraqi society, and certainly work against having the people come together as one nation. Even if the law does not pass, it could be a foreboding of the future.

The thing to remember about Iraq is—ancient as it is—it has really existed for less than 100 years. The nation as it exists today was drawn up by the British after World War I, when the Ottoman Empire (Turkey and parts of central and western Asia) was being dismantled. Many historians make the case that modern Iraq's borders were drawn for political reasons that ultimately reflected British interests at the time, and not necessarily what was prudent for long-term stability. The ethnic and religious mix of Sunni, Shia, and Kurdish people may have been a recipe for disaster, especially in the hands of the ruling Sunni minority elite. Some people charge that the seeds of today's problems were sown at that time, and that an old mistake is simply coming home to roost.

Iraq is a country of great geographic diversity, with mountains in the north, vast deserts in the south, and marshlands along the rivers. The ruggedness of Iraq's terrain is reflected in the people, who have lived through war and poverty, holding on to their families, customs, religious beliefs, and artistic interests. Like people everywhere, Iraqis want peace and a better life for their children. Using that as a unifying theme, perhaps the cradle of civilization can once again achieve the glory of its ancient heritage.

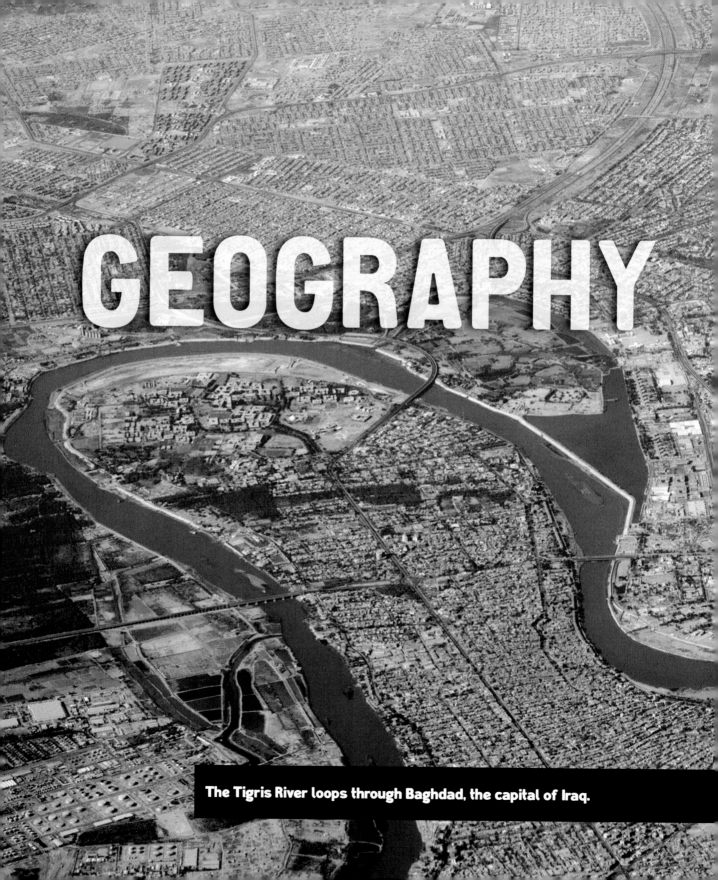

GEOGRAPHY

The Tigris River loops through Baghdad, the capital of Iraq.

1

THE REPUBLIC OF IRAQ HAS A special distinction. It was here, in the lush, life-giving valley between two rivers, that human civilization first arose many thousands of years ago. The Tigris and the Euphrates rivers still flow through this country, bringing a sense of continuity to a land where today's civilization struggles with upheaval and change.

Mesopotamia–"the land between the rivers"–shares the same root word as hippopotamus ("river horse"). *Potam*, from the Greek *potamós*, means "river;" *mésos* means "between," and *ippos* means "horse."

The city of Duhok, in Iraqi Kurdistan, was a popular tourist destination before the war.

A river cuts through a deep canyon in the mountainous northeastern region of Kurdistan in Iraq.

Iraq is located in southwestern Asia. Its neighbors are Turkey to the north, Syria and Jordan to the west, Iran to the east, and Kuwait and Saudi Arabia to the south. Although Iraq is in the far western part of Asia, the region is called the "Near East," more commonly these days, the "Middle East." The terms are designations invented by Europeans, as the region is located to their east. It includes the Arab-speaking nations of northern Africa, the eastern Mediterranean Sea, and the Persian Gulf.

Iraq is almost completely surrounded by land except for a 36-mile-wide (58 km-wide) outlet at its southeastern tip, where it meets the Persian Gulf. Iraq is 865 miles (2,241 km) long from north to south, and 775 miles (2,008 km) wide at its broadest point. The country has a total land area of around 166,859 square miles (432,162 square km), slightly larger than the state of California.

The name for ancient Iraq, *Mesopotamia*, which means "land between the rivers," describes the valleys of the Tigris River and the Euphrates River. The two rivers begin in the mountains of eastern Turkey and flow past northern Syria before reaching the lower valleys of Iraq. The 1,180-mile (3,057-km) Tigris is fed by rivers flowing from the Zagros Mountains; the 1,740-mile (2,800-km) Euphrates has no tributaries. The well-drained Tigris-Euphrates Valley has many lakes.

GEOGRAPHIC REGIONS

The land between the rivers is called "the Fertile Crescent" because it has supported agriculture for thousands of years. Beyond the fertile valley between the Tigris and Euphrates rivers, the topography and vegetation of Iraq changes drastically. Toward the west and south the landscape transforms into a vast, dry desert; toward the north it becomes a cold, mountainous region.

Only 15 percent of Iraqi land, in the northern foothills and mountains, rises more than 1,500 feet (457 m) above sea level. Most of the country is less than 1,000 feet (305 m) above sea level. The lowest point, at sea level, occurs where the Tigris and Euphrates rivers flow into the Persian Gulf.

THE DELTA The delta makes up the southeastern part of Iraq between the capital city (Baghdad) and the Persian Gulf. The delta is mostly a wide fertile plain. Near the city of Basra, where the marshy Lake Hawr al-Hammar lies south of the Euphrates, many winding waterways form marshlands where "Marsh Arabs" have for a long time lived in reed houses. These marshlands, the largest in the Middle East, shrank drastically in the 1990s when Iraqi President Saddam Hussein drained them as an act of aggression against the people there.

The Tigris and Euphrates converge in the delta on the Shatt al-Arab, which flows into the Persian Gulf. Basra, Iraq's only port city, lies on the banks of the Shatt al-Arab. Part of the Shatt al-Arab forms a boundary between Iran and Iraq. Most Iraqis live in this region, from the rural Marsh Arabs

A Marsh Arab family constructs a traditional reed house in the marshlands south of Basra.

Stone dwellings perch on rocky outcroppings in Rawanduz, a town in the Zagros Mountains near the Iran border.

to the sophisticates of the large cities.

Thousands of years ago, the fertile soil of the Tigris-Euphrates valley encouraged nomads to settle there and establish a civilization. The valley today remains the life source of the Iraqi people. However, the Tigris is also a threat to the capital and other cities; frequent spring floods are diverted to protect the cities and irrigate farmlands.

STEPPE—DESERT PLAINS   The area west of the delta region consists of the steppe-desert plains. Most of this area is part of the arid Syrian Desert.

The vast reaches of the plains are sparsely populated because of the harsh climate and rocky terrain. A few channels from the Euphrates run through this region, but they are dry for most of the year. In the southwest, the rocky Al-Hajara Desert extends into Saudi Arabia; it is a popular stop for Bedouin nomads.

NORTHERN FOOTHILLS   North of the city of Samarra, between the Tigris and Euphrates, lie the northern foothills. This region of grassy plains and rolling hills receives generous rainfall. There are few trees, but the foothills produce an abundance of grain. This area has cooler summers and colder winters than the delta region. The foothills are the site of many archaeological ruins, including the ancient city of Assyria.

NORTHEASTERN MOUNTAINS   This region is inhabited mainly by the Kurds, a non-Arab people. The Zagros Mountains rise north of the cities of Mosul and Kirkuk and extend into Iran and Turkey. The terrain consists of mountains, valleys, terraced hills, and pastures. Located here is Iraq's highest mountain, Haji Ibrahim, which stands at 11,891 feet (3,624 m).

The Kurds live in the valleys and foothills of the Zagros Mountains where they cultivate the land. The region has some of Iraq's richest oil fields. However, being so remote, the mountains are also a haven for rebels and criminals.

CLIMATE

Iraq's climate varies dramatically. The north is hot in summer and freezing cold in winter; the east and southeast are tropical and very humid; and the west is desert and very dry. On average, nationwide summer temperatures range from 72°F (24°C) to 110°F (43°C), while temperatures in winter dip to near freezing in the north and to 60°F (16°C) in the south.

The summer season, between June and September, is the hottest time of the year, when Iraq is visited by a northwesterly wind, the *sharqi* (SHAHR-kee). The sharqi is a dry and dusty wind that is often accompanied by dust storms. The scorching sun produces high temperatures of up to 120°F (49°C)

An Iraqi boy makes his way through a flooded street after a heavy rain in Baghdad in November 2013.

Women load reeds into a canoe in the marshlands of southern Iraq.

along the Persian Gulf. In the winter months, from December through March, the southern parts are visited by the *shamal* (shah-MAHL), a cool and moist wind blowing from the sea.

Iraq is a dry country with relatively little rainfall. Much of the rain falls in the winter and spring months, while summers are hot and dry. The annual rainfall is about 16 inches (103 cm) in the delta region and 20 to 40 inches (129 to 258 cm) in the northern foothills and in the mountains. Rain evaporates quickly in the delta, so Iraqis depend on irrigation to cultivate the soil. Destructive floods can occur in the rare event of heavy rainfall.

FLORA

Alpine plants grow in the higher altitudes of Iraq such as the Zagros Mountains. Alpine plants can withstand the freezing winters. Hawthorn, juniper, maple, and oak trees also thrive in the mountains. However, excessive logging has led to the loss of some oak forests.

Vegetation is fairly sparse, largely because of the arid climate and the high salt content of the soil. Desert flora such as the rockrose and storksbill survive the dry summer months and bloom in spring after the rains. Iraq's desert flora is similar to the vegetation in Arizona and New Mexico. Orange and lemon trees grow in central and southern Iraq.

Dates, a dark and extremely sweet fruit, grow on palm trees in many parts of Iraq. Dates are used in a variety of dishes, especially desserts. Other parts of the date palm are also useful. For example, palm fronds are used for weaving, and date pits are ground into a beverage. Because the date palm is so useful, Iraqis refer to it as "the eternal plant" or "the tree of life." Iraq was one of the world's largest exporters of dates in the 1970s. It had some 30 million date palms producing 1.1 million tons (1 million tonnes) of dates

CIVILIZATION BEGAN HERE

Early humans first migrated out of Africa into Asia probably between 2 million and 1.8 million years ago. For hundreds of thousands of years, they lived as hunter-gatherers, finding their food in nature, and wandering in search of more food and shelter as conditions changed. In this way, the earliest people eventually spread across the globe. It wasn't until groups of people learned to grow their own food, and had to stay in one place from one season to the next to harvest what they had sown, that civilizations arose.

As larger groups of people lived together in one place, individuals had to learn specialized tasks. People had to learn cooperation and planning. With that came a hierarchy of power: someone had to give the orders, others had to carry out those orders. Social status emerged, and rules were established. Rules became laws. Records had to be kept, and numbering and writing systems developed in order to keep them. People made music and art, told stories, and developed rituals and belief systems. They domesticated animals, built houses, and made objects. Trade developed and money systems were created. Villages grew and became urban centers.

All of this didn't happen overnight. It didn't even happen over the course of a few years or generations. Civilization was a very gradual process, spurred by the need to survive.

Archaeological excavations of the region between the Tigris and Euphrates rivers, in the south of today's Iraq, began in the 1840s CE. Those digs revealed ruined buildings, clay tablets, and pottery from the ancient Sumerian civilization dating to 3500 BCE. These were the remains of the world's oldest cities—Ur, Eridu, Uruk, Lagash, and Nippur.

annually. But Saddam Hussein's war with Iran and other military campaigns, coupled with decades of neglect, greatly damaged the industry. The country is left with half the number of trees, producing about 463,000 tons (420,000 tonnes).

Reeds grow in marshes and swamps along the Tigris and Euphrates. These plants are used by the cosmetics, pharmaceutical, and food industries. Buttercup and saltbrush grow in the plains and marshlands.

FAUNA

Iraq has relatively little wildlife for its size. One of the most common animals in Iraq is the camel, which can survive on very little water while traveling great distances. The camel has been domesticated to transport heavy loads across the desert.

Iraq's vast deserts may seem to be void of life by day, but at night they come alive as a variety of nocturnal animals emerge from their shady daytime holes. Two common kinds of desert creatures are lizards and snakes. Other

A stork carries material to build a nest. Storks often nest on rooftops in Iraq.

wild desert fauna include hyenas, jackals, and gazelles. Predators such as bears, leopards, foxes, wild boars, and wolves roam the mountainous regions of northern Iraq.

The Tigris and Euphrates rivers contain freshwater fish that people catch for food. Birds such as ducks and geese are found near rivers or swampy marshes. Birds of prey include vultures, eagles, and buzzards. A common bird in Iraq is the stork, which often nests on the roofs of houses. House owners believe they are blessed with luck if a stork nests on their roof.

CITIES

Rapid urbanization in the last fifty years has seen more people moving to the cities. Between 1975 and 2000, Baghdad's population grew by more than 70 percent. About 66.5 percent of Iraqis now live in the large cities or the suburbs. Many cities are located near the Tigris or Euphrates.

Baghdad is reflected in the waters of the Tigris River.

BAGHDAD Iraq's capital city is located on the banks of the Tigris in the delta region. It has a population of about 7.2 million. Baghdad was a small village until 762 CE, when it became the new capital of the Abbasid dynasty. By 800 Baghdad had become a center of culture and education. It prospered until 1258, when it was invaded and ransacked by the Mongols, a warlike people from Mongolia in eastern Asia. Baghdad declined steadily in importance until the mid-sixteenth century, when it became part of the Ottoman Empire and once again prospered. In 1920 Baghdad became the capital of Iraq under British rule.

Besides being the center of government, Baghdad is also a major industrial city, with food processing, cement, and oil industries. The city is a beautiful mix of the old and the modern. The Karkh district on the western bank of the Tigris is the modern section, filled with high-rise buildings and

elegant avenues. Many hotels and foreign banks are found here. The Rusafah district, on the eastern bank of the Tigris, is the old part of the city, with narrow, dusty streets and outdoor bazaars.

However, the capital city has suffered a great deal of damage in the past quarter century. Sanctions against Iraq, which were put in place from 1990 to 2003 by the United Nations Security Council, caused the city's infrastructure to deteriorate from lack of resources. Then, during the Gulf Wars that followed, bombing caused tremendous destruction. The main targets of bombing raids by coalition forces were military and government buildings, but many civilian buildings were also destroyed in the process. The city's water, electrical, and sanitation systems are still quite inadequate.

BASRA   Iraq's chief port is 75 miles (194 km) inland from the Persian Gulf. Founded in 636 CE, Basra is now Iraq's second-largest city, with a population of about 2 million. In the 1960s and 1970s, Basra was a major oil-refining center and a major commercial center, exporting Iraq's oil and dates. Basra was badly damaged during the Iraq-Iran war in the 1980s and in the Gulf wars that followed. Today, like much of Iraq, the port city suffers from a decline in services and worn-out infrastructure caused by a lack of economic resources and rampant corruption. City and business officials are hoping that international investment and rebuilding will help Basra get back on its feet.

MOSUL   Iraq's third-largest city is the urban center of northern Iraq. Mosul is located on the western bank of the Tigris in the northeastern

Kurdish region. Most of Mosul's 1.8 million inhabitants are Kurdish or Arab Muslims. There is also a large Christian community. Mosul depends on oil, cotton, grain, fruit, and sheep for trade. Because of the abundance of cotton, weaving is a popular craft in Mosul. As in Basra, business in Mosul suffered during the years of sanctions and wars.

KIRKUK Iraq's fourth-largest city is the most ethnically diverse, with Kurds, Arabs, and Turkmen in residence. Located in northeastern Iraq, this Kurdish city is a major hub for the oil industry. Oil pipelines run from here through Syria, Lebanon, and Turkey to the Mediterranean ports. When sanctions were imposed in 1990, equipment depreciation reduced Kirkuk's oil production to half its capacity. Kirkuk's population of 851,000 is rapidly growing as more people move from the countryside to the cities. Many Kurds who were displaced during the regime of Saddam Hussein have moved back to the area to reclaim the city.

INTERNET LINKS

www.ancient.eu.com/Mesopotamia
Ancient History Encyclopedia
An excellent overview of Mesopotamia with a good map and many internal links.

www.worldatlas.com
World Atlas
(select "Middle East," then "Select a Middle East Country," "Iraq," "Geography")
Excellent maps and geographic facts.

iraqiculture-usa.com/geography
Iraqi Cultural Office, Washington DC
Links to a huge list of many kinds of Iraq maps, many not easily found elsewhere.

HISTORY

The Abu Duluf mosque in Samarra spirals to the sky. It was built in 852 CE.

2

EVIDENCE OF HUMAN SETTLEMENTS in "the land between the rivers" dates as far back as 10,000 BCE. Obviously, Iraq has a very, very long history. Around this time, hunter-gatherers were just beginning to experiment with growing their own food. It was the dawn of agriculture. The story really begins several thousand years later.

The name *Iraq* may date back to the Sumerian city named Uruk. Or it might derive from the Middle Persian word *eraq* or "lowlands."

Babylon reached its zenith during the reign of Nebuchadnezzar II (c. 605-562 BCE). These ruins are the king's huge southern palace in Babylon.

An Assyrian wall carving depicts a "winged genie," a figure found in temples and palaces from that era. The genie often wears a headband and wristband of rosettes.

The world's first known civilization evolved in Iraq around 3500 BCE. By then, the people in this region had invented the wheel and the sailboat. Some of the earliest evidence of this civilization that archaeologists have found are cylinder seals, which people pressed into soft clay to create a signature. In Mesopotamia, as ancient Iraq was called, small city-states arose in the southeastern region, which together made up a civilization called *Sumer*. The name means "land of the civilized kings." This highly advanced society built irrigation canals and pyramid-shaped temples called *ziggurat* (ZIG-goo-raht), and produced weapons and accurate measuring instruments. The Sumerians also developed the earliest writing system, called cuneiform.

Around 2334 BCE, a man named Sargon worked as a gardener to the king of Sumer. Sargon the Great, as he came to be called, seized the throne, and went on to built the city of Akkad to the north. During his reign from 2334 to 2279 BCE, Sargon expanded his Akkadian Empire across all of Mesopotamia, or, as he called it, to "the four corners of the universe." In essence, he created the first multinational empire, which included some sixty-five cities. Sargon designated his daughter Enheduanna as High Priestess of Inanna at the city of Ur. Inanna was the most important of the Sumerian goddesses, the goddess of love, procreation, and war. Enheduanna wrote many poems in honor of Inanna, and is recognized today as the world's first writer known by name.

A few centuries later, during the Third Dynasty of the city of Ur (2047-1750 BCE), Sumer reached a cultural high point. Technology and art flourished. The Sumerians developed a *sexigesimal* system of counting—a system based on the number sixty—and applied it to the concept of time. They created the sixty-second minute and the sixty-minute hour, and also divided the night and day into periods of twelve hours.

The Babylonians conquered Mesopotamia in 1900 BCE and ruled until 1600 BCE. The most famous Babylonian ruler, King Hammurabi, unified the city-states and created the first known comprehensive code of law.

The last great civilization in Mesopotamia was the Assyrian empire, which lasted from the ninth to the seventh century BCE. The Assyrians were headed by a ruthless monarchy that controlled Mesopotamia and neighboring Syria. Besides their might in war, the Assyrians were known for their great monuments, as excavations at Nineveh, Ashur, Khorsabad, and other sites have shown. By the early seventh century BCE, revolts by the Chaldeans of southern Sumer had ended Assyrian rule. Nebuchadnezzar II, the most famous Chaldean king, who reigned from 605 to 562 BCE, was known not only for his military victories but also for the magnificence of his capital, Babylon.

Young Iraqis stand on top of ruins in Borsippa.

FOREIGN CONQUESTS

After the Chaldeans, a new history in Mesopotamia began as foreign civilizations invaded and conquered the country. The first invaders were the Persians, who conquered the region and added it to their empire in 550 BCE. The area remained under Persian rule until Alexander the Great conquered it in 331 BCE. The Greeks introduced metropolitan cities and scientific rationalism, and improved irrigation systems, trade, and commerce. Alexander had wonderful plans to restore the old temples of Babylon but died of malaria at the young age of thirty-two. His successors were weak, and the Greeks lost Mesopotamia to the Persian Parthians in 126 BCE.

For about 300 years, Mesopotamia was controlled by the Parthians, migrants from Turkestan and northern Iraq. The invaders were true fighters, who overthrew Greek rule but preserved the cities and Greek culture. For brief periods, from 116 CE to 117 CE and again from 198 to 217, the Romans occupied Mesopotamia. The Parthians regained control until 224, when the Iranian Sassanids swept in from the east.

One of the most important conquests occurred in 637, when followers of Prophet Muhammad led troops into Mesopotamia and converted the people to Islam. By 650 the Sassanids had been defeated and Iraq had become the Islamic state it is today.

THE GOLDEN AGE

A great period in Iraqi and Islamic history occurred during the Abbasid caliphate from 750 to 1258, led by the descendants of Prophet Muhammad. Under the Abbasids, Iraq experienced a golden age. The capital city, Baghdad, was organized in three concentric circles: civilians lived in the outer ring, the army in the second ring, and the rulers in the center. The capital became the center of political power and culture in the Middle East, and the country became an important trading center between Asia and the Mediterranean Sea.

This period of glory has become known as the "Golden Age" of Islamic civilization. Baghdad became the home of many new buildings and monuments—mosques, museums, hospitals, and libraries. Scholars from across the Muslim world convened here to study and work. They made important contributions in astronomy, medicine, mathematics, chemistry, literature, and more.

Baghdad reached its peak during the reign of the caliph Harun al-Rashid in the eighth century. The collection of Arab folktales called *A Thousand and One Nights* was written during this time. In the ninth century, Arabic numerals and a decimal system were invented, irrigation systems improved, and diplomatic relations with other states established. By the tenth century, however, the caliphate's influence had declined, as the caliphs focused too much on the cities and too little on the rural areas.

In 1258 Iraq was overrun by Mongol hordes streaming down the plains

SHIA AND SUNNI MUSLIMS

In the religion of Islam, there are two main denominations—Sunni and Shia. In the Muslim world and in most Muslim countries, Sunnis make up the majority. In Iraq, however, Shia Muslims, or Shiites (SHE-ites) are the most populous.

The difference between the two factions dates to 632 CE, the year the Prophet Muhammad died in Saudi Arabia. Muhammad is the founder of Islam. After the Prophet died, there was disagreement among his followers as to who should succeed him. This dispute eventually led to the formation of the two branches of Islam.

All Muslims believe there is one God, Allah, and that Muhammad was Allah's messenger and last prophet. They believe the Qur'an, Islam's holy book, to be the divine word of Allah, as revealed to Muhammad. However, the two sects have different religious interpretations, traditions, and customs. These differences also occasionally translate into political conflicts. (For the sake of understanding, the two branches of Islam can be broadly compared to the various sects in Christianity—Roman Catholicism and Protestantism, or even the various Protestant sects.)

In Iraq, the Sunni have traditionally held power, even though the Shiites make up the majority. After the fall of Saddam Hussein, this discrepancy of power fueled political turmoil that has, on occasion, erupted into violence. After the death of Saddam, and during the U.S. occupation, sectarian hostility calmed and Iraq began to put itself back together. However, since 2013–2014, bloodshed and bombings have once again become more prevalent.

of Central Asia. They destroyed Baghdad and killed the last Abbasid caliph. To this day many Iraqis believe that Iraq never truly recovered from the destruction inflicted by the Mongols. Iraq remained a neglected part of the Mongol empire until 1534, when the Turks seized it and made it a part of the Ottoman Empire.

WORLD WAR I

In 1917, during World War I, the British invaded and captured Baghdad from the Turks. By 1918 they had invaded Mosul and claimed all of Iraq, except the Kurdish region in the north. The British were determined to limit German influence in the Middle East. The British feared that the German alliance with Turkey would disrupt oil lines between Britain, the Middle East, and India. The Arabs cooperated with the British in fighting the Turks on the promise of eventual independence.

In 1920 a British mandate created an Iraqi state. The Iraqis, realizing that they had still not reached their goal of total independence, organized a number of revolts. In 1922 Britain agreed to grant Iraq independence by 1932.

INDEPENDENCE AND MONARCHY

In October 1932, Iraq was admitted to the League of Nations as an independent monarchy. Independent Iraq faced many problems internally and with neighboring countries. King Faisal ruled Iraq until his death in 1933.

Young King Faisal II only ruled for five years before being executed by revolutionaries.

Faisal's son, Ghazi, was unable to pull the divided country together. Ghazi's rule was interrupted by a military coup, yet he stayed in control until his death in an automobile accident in 1939. After Ghazi's death, his infant son, Faisal II, became the new ruler of Iraq. Faisal II's uncle, Amir Abd al-Ilah, acted as regent until the boy was old enough to rule.

Faisal II was the king of Iraq between 1953 and 1958. During his reign, Iraq suffered from the aftermath of World War II and political misjudgment. In the late 1940s, the economy plummeted due to worldwide shortages and a mass exodus of affluent Jews from Iraq to the newly-established nation of Israel.

On July 14, 1958, an uproar began in the streets of Baghdad as the people of Iraq revolted against the monarchy. The revolutionaries, led by General Abdul Karim Kassem, publicly executed King Faisal II, Amir Abd al-Ilah, and other members of the royal family. This revolution was one in a series of military coups that plagued Iraq until the successful retention of power by the *Baath* (bah-AHTH) Party in 1968.

THE ERA OF SADDAM HUSSEIN BEGINS

In 1963 the Kassem regime was replaced by the Baath Party, which organized a military coup that lasted less than a year. The party's lack of definitive programs and leaders permitted the Nasserites, a group led by Abd as-Salaam Arif, who had played a leading role in the 1958 revolution, to overthrow them.

In 1966 Arif was killed in a helicopter crash. His militarily weak brother, Abd ar-Rahman Arif, became president. In 1968 a highly organized and militarily strong Baath Party dominated by Ahmad Hassan al-Bakr and Saddam Hussein overthrew President Arif and took control of Iraq.

Al-Bakr became the president of Iraq, and Hussein the vice president and deputy secretary general of the Baath Party. In 1979 al-Bakr resigned, and Hussein became president.

Saddam Hussein threatens Iran in this photo from 1980.

THE IRAQ-IRAN WAR

In 1979 in Iran underwent a revolution. Iran is Iraq's huge neighbor to the east. The *ayatollah* (Shiite religious leader) Sayyid Ruhollah Musavi Khomeini overthrew the Western-leaning shah, or king, of Iran. In his place, Khomeini established a new Shia-led government and declared Iran to be an Islamic republic.

Saddam Hussein, a Sunni Muslim, feared that Iran would agitate a rebellion among the Shia Muslims in Iraq. Although the Shia were a majority in Iraq, the Sunni were the ruling elite—the ones with the political power. Saddam sent his troops into Iran for a full-scale war. This was also a means for Hussein to gain full control of the Shatt al-Arab and of the oil-producing Iranian border province of Khuzestan. The war lasted eight years, incurred an estimated total economic loss of $1.2 billion, and claimed the lives of a million Iraqis and Iranians.

Iraqi troops flash victory signs as they roll past a crushed tank on their way to the front line in 1985 during the Iraq-Iran war.

The Iraq-Iran War began on September 22, 1980. Due to the political changes in Iran at the time, Iraq had invaded a disorganized Iran. In the first few months of the bitter war, Iraqi forces laid siege to several Iranian towns and killed hundreds of troops.

The Iranians gathered strength and retaliated in the spring of 1982, forcing the Iraqis to retreat. Underestimating the new strength of the Iranian troops, Hussein attempted to settle the war. The bitter Iranians refused his peace offering and launched a massive offensive. They came very close to capturing the Iraqi port city of Basra, which the Iraqis defended at a huge cost to human life.

In 1986 the Iraqis used chemical weapons in the war, killing tens of thousands of Iranian troops. With increased military aid from the West, Iraq gained the upper hand. Iran, realizing that the tide of war was turning against it, agreed to a ceasefire in August 1988. Neither side emerged victorious. For both countries, the war was a tragedy with enormous social and economic consequences.

THE 1991 GULF WAR

In the aftermath of the Iraq-Iran war, the Iraqi economy was devastated. With depressed oil prices affecting Iraq's revenue, Hussein turned his attention to Kuwait.

Several blown-out wells burn in the Al-Ahmadi oil field in Kuwait. In 1991, Iraqi troops, retreating after a seven-month occupation of Kuwait, smashed and torched 727 wells, badly polluting the atmosphere and creating crude oil lakes.

Hussein and the Al Sabah family ruling the Kuwaiti emirate had a number of disagreements, such as the oil fields lying on the disputed Iraq-Kuwait border. The border had been a source of friction since 1958, when Iraq became a republic, as various regimes in Baghdad since then had laid claim to Kuwait.

On August 2, 1990, Hussein ordered his troops to invade Kuwait. In a matter of hours, the ruling Al Sabah family fled to exile in Saudi Arabia. The worldwide reaction to the invasion was swift. The United Nations imposed economic sanctions on Iraq that rendered the country unable to export its oil and that halted imports into Iraq and froze Iraqi assets overseas. A military alliance formed predominantly by the United States and Britain that included troops from Middle Eastern nations, other European nations, and Australia started gathering in the deserts of Saudi Arabia close to the Iraq-Kuwait border.

The United Nations passed a resolution in December 1990 authorizing the use of force against Iraq unless its troops withdrew from Kuwait by January 15, 1991. The deadline passed without any Iraqi withdrawal, and the Allies launched an air attack on military installations and government targets in Iraq as well as on the Iraqi garrison in Kuwait. Hussein had Soviet-made planes for air defense, which quickly proved inadequate against the high-tech fighter planes, weapons, and other war apparatus of the coalition forces.

THE SAD TALE OF THE BAGHDAD ZOO

When war came to Baghdad in 2003, it brought death, destruction, and deep suffering ... to the helpless inhabitants of the city zoo. In some ways, the sad tale of what happened at the Baghdad Zoo is a metaphor for the story of Iraq itself.

The 200-acre Baghdad Zoo had been the largest zoo in the Middle East, home to more than 600 animals. However, conditions at the zoo were poor. By modern standards, the animal enclosures were small and inadequate; many were merely cages with bars and concrete floors. Economic sanctions in the years leading up to the 2003 invasion had seriously impacted the zookeepers' abilities to buy food and medicines for the animals.

Even before the U.S.-led forces arrived in Bagdad, troops loyal to Saddam Hussein took up defensive positions in the zoo itself. The dangerous situation forced the zookeepers to stay away, and the animals were left alone, locked in their cages, unfed and dying of thirst. Meanwhile, people in Baghdad were starving as well, and looters broke into the abandoned zoo. They stole many of the animals and ate them, including the zoo's two giraffes.

Then the real fighting started. A mortar attack hit the lion enclosure, leaving a gaping hole in the wall. A couple of starving lions escaped, and one attacked a horse. A brown bear escaped into the city and killed three Iraqis. U.S. soldiers tried to round up the wandering animals, including a baboon that had found its way into the desert. But by then, only thirty five animals remained alive in the Baghdad Zoo.

South African conservationist Lawrence Anthony rushed to Baghdad. There, he worked with U.S. Army Captain William Sumner to rescue, protect, and rehabilitate the animals and the zoo itself. International conservation organizations worked with them and the zoo reopened three months later with eighty-six animals, including many found at Hussein family compounds and private zoos.

Today the zoo has grown. It has 1000 animals of seventy species, many of them donated from other zoos around the world. The story of the zoo has inspired several books including Babylon's Ark: The Incredible Wartime Rescue of the Baghdad Zoo *by Lawrence Anthony and Graham Spence (2007) and a play,* Bengal Tiger at the Baghdad Zoo *by Rajiv Joseph, which premiered in 2009.*

Riley and Hope are two Bengal tigers donated to the zoo by a U.S. conservation group to aid in its restoration.

On February 24, the Allies moved into Kuwait with minimal Iraqi resistance; what was left of the Iraqi forces in Kuwait retreated to Iraq or surrendered. On February 28, 1991, a ceasefire was signed at Safwan in southern Iraq. Hussein claimed that the war was a victory for Iraq, even though 100,000 Iraqis had died. Acts of sabotage by the retreating Iraqis caused terrible damage to Kuwait's oil fields and sea lanes.

In 2003, the United States invaded Iraq, engaging in a new war—called the Iraq War or the Second Gulf War—and put an end to the regime of Saddam Hussein. And so began a new phase in the long, tumultuous, and sometimes barbarically uncivilized history of "the cradle of civilization."

INTERNET LINKS

www.factmonster.com
Click on "World" and then select country, "Iraq"
Alternatively, go directly to:
www.factmonster.com/ipka/A0107644.html
FactMonster
An excellent site for secondary school students. The history of Iraq includes an in-depth look at the recent wars and U.S.-led occupation.

www.metmuseum.org/toah/ht/?period=06&region=wam
Heilbrunn Timeline of Art History:
"Iraq (Mesopotamia) 500—1000 A.D."
This excellent interactive timeline from the Metropolitan Museum of Art in New York highlights historical events and works of art.

www.poetryinternationalweb.net/pi/site/poem/item/14246/poem_ org_audio/THE-BAGHDAD-ZOO
Read and listen to "The Baghdad Zoo," a poem by Iraq war veteran Brian Turner, from his book of poetry about the war, *Here, Bullet* (2005).

GOVERNMENT

A demonstrator holds up the national flag at a 2012 rally in Basra, demanding better living conditions and an end to corruption.

3

GOVERNING A COUNTRY IN TURMOIL is a great challenge. But more than that, it can be like a race against time. Since the U.S. invasion in 2001, the final demise of Saddam Hussein in 2006, and the subsequent withdrawal of U.S. troops in 2011, the Iraqis have struggled to establish a stable government. In the midst of that effort, factions of the Iraqi population have differing visions for their nation. Opposition to the existing government has spurred violence that threatens to break into civil war. Under such conditions, it is uncertain what form the Iraqi government will ultimately take.

Today Iraq has a post-war government in place that is still trying to recover from the Saddam Hussein years. Forces loyal to Hussein maintained order by relying heavily on repression in the forms of imprisonment, torture, and murder. Of the twenty-three ministries, the largest government agency was the Ministry of the Interior, which consisted of the police and the militia, whose forces numbered far greater than those of the army.

"We do know that the democratic experience in Iraq is . . . fragile, but it was born very strong. . . . Democracy needs to be strong, and we are going to strengthen it because it only will allow us to fight terrorism."
–Iraq Prime Minister Nouri al-Maliki, November 2013

But in 2003 all that changed. After the first Gulf War in 1991, Iraq operated under sanctions imposed by the United Nations that strictly limited Iraq's trade with other countries. Iraq could not sell its oil in the international market; nor could it receive any goods except medical necessities.

Even with black-market trading and the fact that some medical products were allowed under the sanctions, many of the people of Iraq were deprived of lifesaving—and even basic—medical care, as well as food and other products needed to sustain life. Many other Iraqis, especially those favored by the Baath Party, lived very well despite international pressure.

After the first Gulf War the international community attempted by various means—sanctions, restrictions, and inspections—to determine if the government of Saddam Hussein was manufacturing what they referred to as "weapons of mass destruction." These weapons were thought to include a variety of chemical weapons—poisons that could be spread through the air or water. Although weapons of this sort had been internationally outlawed since World War I, Saddam Hussein had used them against Iran and against the Kurdish people of northern Iraq.

Saddam Hussein's Al-Faw Palace in Baghdad, also known as the Water Palace, became the headquarters of the occupying multinational forces during Operation Iraqi Freedom.

IRAQ REFUSES TO COOPERATE

Repeatedly the United Nations sent inspectors to Iraq to examine manufacturing sites and other places that they thought might be used to make or store weapons of mass destruction. The inspectors failed to find any, but were rarely free to determine their own course of investigation or to speak freely with those who might have had knowledge of the matter. Inspectors often had reason to suspect that representatives from the Iraqi government were being less than helpful. At times, they found conditions or materials that suggested weapons had been made or stored in the past, but they could not say so with certainty.

The international response to Iraq's level of cooperation was generally negative. But there was disagreement about how much danger Saddam Hussein and his activities actually posed and, more importantly, what should be done about it. After the terrorist attacks on the United States in September 2001, the administration of U.S. president George W. Bush said

"All the decades of deceit and cruelty have now reached an end. Saddam Hussein and his sons must leave Iraq within forty-eight hours. Their refusal to do so will result in military conflict, commenced at a time of our choosing."
–George W. Bush, March 17, 2003

In February 2003, President Saddam Hussein, seated right, chairs a meeting with high-ranking Iraqi officials, including his son Qusai, second left, head of the elite Republican Guard.

Saddam Hussein posed an intolerable risk. Relying on intelligence that they claimed showed both proof of the presence of weapons of mass destruction and a connection between Afghanistan's al-Qaeda terrorists and the Iraqi regime, the United States urged further inspections.

Iraq did not cooperate and the U.S. government prepared for war. Some members of the coalition that had fought the first Gulf War—notably France and Germany—opposed going to war at this time. Throughout the world, people took to the streets to demonstrate their opposition to a new war. Protests in the United States and Great Britain were especially heartfelt, but did not deter the two governments from proceeding to war.

THE SECOND GULF WAR (THE IRAQ WAR)

In spring of 2003, the United States and Great Britain prepared to attack Iraq, with the intention of deposing Saddam Hussein and his Baath Party and destroying his cache of weapons of mass destruction. They called their incursion Operation Iraqi Freedom, referring to the second half of the plan for Iraq—to set up a free and democratic government run by the Iraqi

Two U.S. tanks patrol the streets of Baghdad on April 14, 2003.

people. By mid-March hundreds of thousands of British, American, and Australian troops had already made their way to Kuwait, where they amassed on Iraq's border, waiting for orders to invade.

The fighting began in the dark hours before dawn on March 19, 2003. Acting on intelligence that told them that Saddam Hussein and his family were hiding in one of his palaces in Baghdad, the United States launched missiles that targeted and bombed the palace and other sites in the city. At the same time, nearly 200,000 coalition forces began their march to

A medical tank rushes wounded soldiers to medical attention during combat operations in Fallujah, Iraq, in November 2004.

Baghdad in a huge cavalry of tanks and armored personnel carriers. Overhead, planes supplied air cover and bombed key sites in the cities.

The first week of the war was eye-opening for the invading forces as well as the ruling regime. The coalition plan was to avoid most of the populated areas in the south of the country, in the belief that the regime had few supporters there. This would greatly lessen civilian casualties and infrastructural damage. The coalition planned to secure as quickly as possible the southern city of Basra and the roads and bridges they would need to move their troops to Baghdad. However, in this endeavor they were met by seemingly disorganized, but fierce, guerrilla opposition.

Though initially surprised and slowed, the troops made inexorable progress. On April 3 they took over Saddam International Airport and renamed it Baghdad International Airport. On April 9 they declared themselves in control of Baghdad. For three weeks thousands of bombs and guided missiles fell on Baghdad in an unmistakable demonstration of military supremacy. Resistance from the regime's feared Republican Guard troops stationed around Baghdad never materialized.

Turning their attention to northern Iraq, U.S. Special Forces landed in Kurdish-controlled areas, where, aided by Kurdish militias, they took control of the northern oil fields, barely opposed by the Iraqi army.

THE UNTIDY DEATH OF SADDAM HUSSEIN

What happened to Saddam Hussein? When U.S.-led forces entered Baghdad in April 2003, the tyrant, his family, and most senior Iraqi government officials had all disappeared. For the United States, finding Saddam became a top priority and the military set about rounding up anyone who might know his whereabouts. Occasionally Saddam would issue audio tapes in which he called on Iraqis to defy the occupying forces, but he stayed hidden.

After months of gathering information, on December 13, 2003, U.S. operatives descended on a farmhouse near Tikrit in a dramatic raid called Operation Red Dawn. Inside a shack on the property, they found a rough underground chamber, essentially a man-sized hole in the ground. Lying inside it was a bearded and disheveled Saddam Hussein. He was armed with a pistol and an AK-47 assault rifle, and he had a large amount of cash in U.S. dollars. He put up no resistance.

The following summer, the Supreme Iraqi Criminal Tribunal charged Saddam with crimes against humanity. Specific charges included the murder of 148 people, the torture of women and children, and the illegal arrest of 399 others, all having to do with one specific incident in 1982. However, Saddam was alleged to be responsible for many other crimes, including:

- the deaths of thousands of political rivals,
- the use of chemical weapons against the Kurdish population, resulting in some 50,000 to 100,000 deaths,
- the draining of the marshes in southern Iraq in a largely successful attempt to destroy the livelihoods of the Marsh Arabs,
- the invasion of Kuwait and the torching of more than 700 oil wells there, and the deliberate release of a huge quantity of oil into the Persian Gulf.

Saddam was found guilty and on Dec. 30, 2006, he was hanged. In a final blow to the tyrant who had once lived in opulent palaces, Saddam was sent to his death by poorly behaved guards who insulted him and filmed him with their cell phones.

Now all that remained was Tikrit, Hussein's hometown. On April 14 Tikrit fell to U.S. Marines. Sporadic resistance to coalition forces would continue throughout the country, especially in the cities and former Baathist strongholds, but Bush declared the war to be over. Throughout the country the Iraqi people took to the streets to celebrate the fall of Hussein and his ruling party. Statues, posters, paintings, and other trappings of his rule were smashed and burned in the streets. In public, most Iraqis celebrated his passing.

U.S. troops helped jubilant Iraqis topple this statue of Saddam Hussein.

AFTER THE WAR

From the beginning of the war, one goal of the invading nations had been to replace Saddam Hussein. To that end, invading forces avoided as much as possible damaging or destroying infrastructure. Nevertheless, at the end of the conflict, the cities were left in disorder. Desperation and anger drove

THE GOVERNMENT TAKES SHAPE

Under the current constitution, Iraq's federal government is defined as an Islamic, democratic, federal parliamentary republic. It is composed of three branches, the executive, legislative, and judicial, as well as numerous independent commissions. The executive branch is composed of the president, the prime minister, and the Council of Ministers.

In 2010, Iraq held parliamentary elections deciding the 325 members of the Council of Representatives of Iraq, made up of a coalition composed largely of members of four main political parties as well as some representatives of minority parties. This council then elected the prime minister and president. Incumbent Nouri al-Maliki was chosen to continue on as prime minister and head of the government. During the reign of Saddam Hussein, al-Maliki was a Shiite dissident who lived in exile from Iraq from 1979 to 2003, returning when Hussein was overthrown. Incumbent Jalal Talabani was chosen to continue as president of Iraq, and head of state. A leading Kurdish politician, Talabani is the first non-Arab president of Iraq.

Al-Maliki's government is credited with working with the United States toward the withdrawal of U.S. troops, which was largely accomplished in 2011, and with greatly boosting oil production. However, it has been accused of corruption, failing to hem in al-Qaeda and Shiite dissident violence, human rights abuses, and failure to alleviate widespread poverty in Iraq.

Prime Minister Nouri al-Maliki

many to loot former palaces of the elite, and even their own institutions and museums. Some Iraqis who had opposed the regime of Hussein returned from the countries where they had waited out his rule. Some declared themselves political leaders, others religious leaders. But they tended not to remain in power, and there was no clear central government.

The United States appointed its own functionaries to supervise restoring infrastructure services, such as electricity, running water, telephone lines, garbage collection, and sewage treatment. They were also in charge of civil security. The Iraqi people were anxious to resume the everyday activities of life: going to school, shopping, banking, and working and conducting business.

Workers reconstruct buildings in Baghdad that were damaged during the war.

Nevertheless, months after the fall of Hussein's regime, much remained to be done to restore order and safety to Iraq. The interim government was not working smoothly. Millions of people had yet to return to work, though the Americans were paying them salaries anyway so they could feed their families. Potential religious and civil leaders rose to prominence almost daily, competing for the loyalties of a confused populace.

Months turned into years. If the first part of the war—the removal of Saddam Hussein—was won with relative ease, the second part—setting up a free and democratic government run by the Iraqi people—turned out to be extremely difficult, if not impossible. Iraqis increasingly resisted the imposition of outside rule and demanded that the United States keep its promises—a stable government, a better life, and the repair of Iraq's devastated infrastructure. However, these goals proved to be much harder to achieve than the United States had expected.

Who among the Iraqis would emerge to assume leadership? Who could get Iraq's religious, ethnic, and political factions to work together? These groups were diverse and sometimes operated in opposition to each other. Religious groups included Shia Muslims, Sunni Muslims, and Christians. People with ethnic identities and priorities included Arabs, Kurds, Assyrians, and Turkomans. Political contenders included Shia-backed groups supporting an Islamic government, secular organizations favoring a democratically-elected government, and tribal groups, which had traditionally provided order in the

LULLABY FOR THE HUNGRY

by Muhammad Mahdi Al-Jawahiri,
Iraqi poet (1899–1997)

Sleep, You hungry people, sleep!
The gods of food watch over you.
Sleep, if you are not satiated
By wakefulness, then sleep shall fill you.
Sleep, with thoughts of smooth-as butter-
*   promises,*
Mingled with words as sweet as honey.
Sleep, and enjoy the best of health.
What a fine thing is sleep for the
*   wretched!*
Sleep till the resurrection morning
Then it will be time enough to rise.
Sleep in the swamps
Surging with silty waters.
Sleep to the tune of mosquitoes humming
As if it were the crooning of doves.
Sleep to the echo of long speechifyings
By great and eminent power politicians.
Sleep, You hungry people sleep!
For sleep is one of the blessings of peace.
It is stupid for you to rise,
Sowing discord where harmony reigns.
Sleep, for the reform of corruption

Simply consists in your sleeping on.
Sleep, You hungry people, sleep!
Don't cut off others' livelihood.
Sleep, your skin cannot endure
The shower of sharp arrows when you
*   wake.*
Sleep, for the yards of jail houses
Are all teeming with violent death,
And you are the more in need of rest
After the harshness of oppression.
Sleep, and the leaders will find ease
From a sickness that has no cure.
Sleep, You hungry people, sleep!
For sleep is more likely to protect your
*   rights*
And it is sleep that is most conducive
To stability and discipline.
Sleep, I send my greetings to you;
I send you peace, as you sleep on.
Sleep, You hungry people, sleep!
The gods of food watch over you.
Sleep, You hungry people, sleep!
The gods of food watch over you.

rural areas. Into this mix came long-exiled Iraqis, religious and secular, and funding from interests outside Iraq.

As Iraqis struggled to regain their footing in the years following the overthrow of Hussein, the occupying forces found themselves with much to do and no visible end to their responsibility to run Iraq. The Iraqi people looked to their own leaders, to the American administrators, and to themselves for relief, but for everyone the problems were many and the solutions uncertain.

Iraqi militants brandish their weapons in Fallujah in January 2014.

INTERNET LINKS

www.cia.gov/library/publications/the-world-factbook/geos/iz.html
CIA World Factbook: Iraq
An overview of facts and statistics.

www.iraqiembassy.us
Embassy of the Republic of Iraq, Washington, D.C.
This official website features up-to-date news, videos, and photo galleries.

new.krg.us
Kurdistan Regional Government, Iraq
News and information about the autonomous Kurdistan region of Iraq.

www.npr.org/series/4962517/saddam-hussein-crimes-and-punishment
NPR: Saddam Hussein: Crimes and Punishment
An audio series of radio stories from November and December 2006 about the death of Saddam Hussein.

ECONOMY

Watermelons from Syria are stacked for sale along a main road in Baghdad. In 2013, the price of the melons more than doubled.

4

THREE DECADES OF WAR AND government mismanagement have badly hurt Iraq's economy. Ongoing criminal and terrorist violence makes international investors wary of doing business in the country. Tourism, which could be an economic boon for Iraq, with its rich art and archaeological history, is extremely limited for the same reason. Even if violence wasn't a factor, tourist facilities such as hotels, museums, and other attractions, are in poor condition, if they exist at all.

When oil became Iraq's principal industry in the first half of the twentieth century, the Iraqi economy surged. Iraq became one of the world's leading producers of oil, generating significant revenue. The economy prospered in the 1970s, as oil production rose to its peak toward the end of the decade.

In the 1980s the Iraq-Iran War interrupted economic development in Iraq. Oil revenues fell, as oil wells and refineries were destroyed in battle, and the cost of waging war put a great strain on the economy. Iraq spent $35 billion of its reserves financing the eight-year war. By 1988 Iraq had accumulated a debt of $50 billion and the economy hit rock bottom. After Iraq invaded Kuwait in 1990, the international

In Iraq, over 80 percent of farmers practice traditional farming techniques that result in low production and productivity. The country's Ministry of Agriculture hopes to educate farmers on modern, more efficient methods, such as furrow irrigation instead of flood irrigation, which will help farmers cope with water shortages.

community imposed sanctions restricting Iraqi trade with other nations. This was a devastating blow to the economy, as Iraq depended heavily on oil export revenues.

THE OIL INDUSTRY

The British discovery of oil in Iran in 1908 spurred similar explorations in Iraq. In 1927 the British- and U.S.-controlled Turkish Petroleum Company discovered a rich oil well near the northern city of Kirkuk. The Turkish Petroleum Company was renamed the Iraq Petroleum Company and was granted a 70-year exploration contract by the Iraqi government. By 1938 oil had become Iraq's major export commodity.

After World War II, Basra and Mosul became popular oil-drilling sites. By 1951 Basra, Mosul, and Kirkuk were exporting almost 20 million tons of oil annually. Upset by the revenue earned by foreign companies, the Iraqi government demanded 50 percent of all oil profits.

An Iraqi worker operates valves at a refinery near the Nahran Omar oil field in Basra.

The Iraq Petroleum Company continued to operate in Iraq until 1973, when the government nationalized the oil companies, paying $300 million for the shares of the Iraq Petroleum Company. The government set up a Ministry of Oil and established the Iraqi National Oil Company, which assumed responsibility for the management of oil production in the country.

Iraq is a member of the Organization of Petroleum Exporting Countries (OPEC), formed in 1960 to control petroleum prices worldwide. In the 1970s OPEC reduced its oil exports, triggering severe oil shortages and skyrocketing oil prices in the United States and other countries that depended on oil imports. OPEC lost some of its influence in the 1980s when attempts to control the world's oil supply failed as countries such as Mexico and the Soviet Union began exporting oil.

Iraq has one of the largest proven oil and natural gas reserves in the world. Its oil reserves are estimated at 140.3 billion barrels, and its natural gas reserves at 112.6 trillion cubic feet (3.19 trillion cubic m.), the tenth largest in the world.

Iraq's output began to expand in 2010 after it secured service contracts with giant oil companies such as BP, Shell, Eni, and Exxon Mobil. Today, Iraq is OPEC's second-largest oil producer and its fastest growing producer. Unlike other parts of Iraq's economy, the oil industry has been robust going into 2014. Forecasters expect to see continued growth in this sector unless political and security problems get in the way, which is a strong possibility.

AGRICULTURE

Iraq has been an agricultural nation since ancient times. In the 1970s half the Iraqi labor force was engaged in agriculture, but the emphasis on agriculture

Dates hang from a date palm in bunches. Dates are one of Iraq's most important export products.

A grocer prepares crates of olives for sale.

waned as oil became the primary contributor to the country's economy. Today about 20 percent of Iraqis farm the land, but this figure is falling.

Less than 15 percent of Iraq's land area, mostly in the northeastern plains and mountain valleys, is farmed. The main crops in the delta and plains region are wheat, barley, corn, rice, and fruit. Most of the farmland here is near the Tigris and Euphrates, which provide water for crops. In the northeast, with higher rainfall, tobacco, barley, olives, and fruit are grown. Dates are the largest agricultural export and the second largest foreign currency earner after oil. However, date production fell after the first Gulf War, when oil pollution affected millions of trees in the south.

Before the first Gulf War, Iraq imported 70 percent of its food. Under trade sanctions, food imports were restricted and the agricultural sector raised production but could not meet the demand. As with so much else, Iraq's food production has not yet recovered from the decades of war and sanctions and Iraq still suffers food shortages.

WATER RESOURCES

For thousands of years, the Tigris and Euphrates rivers have irrigated the land yet also brought destruction. The ancient Sumerian civilization had a myth about these rivers flooding so far that the waters covered large parts of Mesopotamia.

In the last century, Iraq has developed the means to control the flow of the rivers. Several dams in Iraq collect and store floodwater to distribute it to farms during the dry season. The dams once bolstered Iraq's economy by reducing flood damage, supporting agriculture, and generating electricity.

Today the water situation is troublesome. Some of the dams and hydroelectric projects built during the Saddam Hussein regime caused

severe damage downstream to Iraq's marshlands, in the delta region of the great rivers. Environmentalists around the world insist that the marshland problem must be rectified. Further complicating Iraq's water problems, Turkey—Iraq's neighbor to the north—has been developing its own massive program of water projects. The Southeastern Anatolia Project (GAP) is one of the largest river basin development projects in the world. Both the Tigris and the Euphrates rivers begin in Turkey and meander through the Taurus Mountains before entering Iraq.

For several decades already, Turkey has been constructing twenty-two new hydroelectric dams and nineteen hydroelectric power plants on both the Tigris and the Euphrates. Upon completion it is expected to provide up to 25 percent of Turkey's electricity. When the project is complete, it could reduce the quantity of water flowing in the two rivers by 70 to 80 percent. The quality of the water is also being affected. As the rivers flow closer to the Persian Gulf, the level of salinity, or saltiness, has been rising.

Farms along these rivers in Iraq are already drying up, due to these

Water projects, such as dams and hydroelectric power stations, often cause tensions downstream relating to water shortages.

A woman works in a brick factory in Najaf. Most manual laborers work long hours in harsh conditions for low wages.

problems and the aggravating factor of recent drought. Since 2005, water shortages have prompted 100,000 Iraqis to move from their native communities.

MANUFACTURING

Manufacturing was once the backbone of the Iraqi economy, but after years of sanctions and war, Iraqi manufacturers are no longer able to compete with other foreign producers. Today thousands of factories are boarded up or have been converted to warehouses. Government officials want to improve the country's manufacturing capacity. They are eager to attract investment in many areas: petrochemicals, construction, textiles, food, drugs, fertilizers, vehicles, cement, ceramics, paper products, and many others. But progress has been slow.

TRANSPORTATION

During the 1980s the government invested heavily to improve the transportation system. Winding dirt

eline

onal

y primitive until the 1960s—a standard Syrian border, and a meter gauge line asures the width of the railway line.) was a great hindrance in transporting nding from the former Soviet Union, asra to Baghdad, Mosul, Kirkuk, Syria,

The Baghdad Central Station was badly damaged in the war.

iraq
n presents a quick overview of Iraq's

10-24/surging-bloodshed-ny.html
dercut Iraq's Oil-Fueled Economy."

ness stories about Iraq.

ENVIRONMENT

An oil covered seabird suffers as a result of the deliberate oil spill by Iraqi soldiers during the 1991 Persian Gulf War in Kuwait.

5

THE IRAQI PEOPLE ARE NOT THE only ones who suffered under Saddam Hussein. Iraq's land and wildlife were devastated as well. Multiple wars, twelve years of economic sanctions, and general mismanagement have taken a toll on the environment.

On top of other problems, Iraq's environment is particularly vulnerable to global climate change. Changing weather patterns are increasing extreme weather events, such as flash flooding in some areas, and sand or dust storms in others. Meanwhile drought and desertification dry up Iraq's already scarce water resources.

Litter pollutes a tributary of the Shatt al-Arab waterway in Basra.

NATURE, A VICTIM OF WAR

While the loss of human life is the most painful consequence of war, the loss of plant and animal life due to war also has serious implications. Iraq's terrain consists mainly of desert, mountains, and marshlands. Located in the northern part of the gulf, the country is an important area for migratory and endemic birds, including around fifteen threatened species. Iraq's birdlife includes the greater flamingo, white-headed duck, and Basra reed warbler, which is native to Iraq.

The war with Iran from 1980 to 1988 polluted marshlands where wetland birds spend winter. During the first Gulf War, following Iraq's invasion of Kuwait, allied bombing and tank tracking destroyed great expanses of vegetation in the Iraqi desert. Millions of barrels of crude oil spilled into the Persian Gulf blackened surrounding coasts and killed marine life.

The short war in 1991 generated long-term environmental damage,

Children play with unexploded tank shells in Tell Billa, Iraq.

but before the land could recover from its effects, in 2003 a second Gulf War erupted.

Desertification is another adverse effect of war on the land. Military activity speeds up the process of desert expansion. Tank tracks and bomb explosions crush and burn desert flora and pollute the sands with oil and debris, while toxins released from weapons of war poison groundwater.

During the first Gulf War, the allied forces hit water and sewage treatment plants in Iraq. As a result, the Iraqis were deprived of clean drinking water, and waste water and garbage flooded the streets. Such conditions led to outbreaks of waterborne diseases, such as typhoid, from which thousands suffered and died. After more than a decade of sanctions, even as the second Gulf War loomed, Baghdad's water and sewage treatment facilities were still in a poor state, and some streets were still blocked and flooded.

Iraq's landscape is littered with the debris of war.

Buildings, including schools and homes, and environmental and archaeological sites were destroyed during the 2003 Gulf War. A lack of finances and a glut of social and health problems have hindered repairs

OIL SPILLS

In 1991, as Iraqi soldiers retreated from Kuwait, they released millions of barrels of crude oil into the Persian Gulf to hold off coalition forces. The oil blackened the gulf coast, staining beaches not just in Kuwait but in neighboring nations as well. The oil poisoned or suffocated thousands of fish and waterbirds, and it was predicted that toxins from oil residues might continue to affect fisheries in the gulf for a hundred years. In terms of volume of oil released into the waters, it was the worst oil spill in history—all the worse because it was deliberate.

In 2003, a bomb explosion damaged an oil pipeline northwest of Baghdad. The leaking oil polluted this date palm grove.

With help from its neighbors and from the United States and other nations, the Kuwaiti government spent millions of dollars cleaning up after the oil spills. As the Second Gulf War loomed in 2003, pollution-control companies went on the alert to organize cleanup crews in the event of a similar ecological disaster, but luckily such an event didn't happen.

OIL FIRES

Oil fires have been a major source of air pollution in Iraq. In 1991 Iraqi troops set oil wells in Kuwait on fire as they retreated. Firefighters took months after the war to stop the fires, which filled the skies over Iraq as well as Kuwait and Saudi Arabia with soot and other toxic particles. The airborne pollutants mixed with water vapor and formed clouds of acid rain. The oil fires also produced high levels of carbon dioxide, with possible climate change consequences. (Carbon dioxide contributes to the greenhouse effect in the atmosphere.)

Massive cleanup efforts lasted a decade, but the oil fires, oil mists, and acid rains had already done irreversible damage to the air, causing respiratory problems among people and poisoning plants and animals.

HEALTH MATTERS

An oil-well fire burns near Taji in 2006.

Iraq's environmental issues are also major health issues. For example, without proper sanitation and clean water, many Iraqis have contracted life-threatening diseases, which the hospitals are unable to treat without adequate and appropriate medical supplies. Certain diseases resulting from unclean drinking water and poor sanitation cause malnutrition among children. For example, sufferers of dysentery are unable to retain food and absorb essential nutrients.

The hospitals are even less equipped to treat patients during wartime, when there are more and worse cases, such as severe burns, because access to medical and surgical supplies is more difficult on the battlefield.

Land near the Iraq—Iran border is plagued with landmines laid in the 1980s that did not explode during the war and still lie in the earth like ticking time bombs. For Iraqis living near the border, stepping on a landmine is a daily possibility. Landmines in Iraq have maimed or killed many people, such as Bedouin nomads. In 2009, according to the U.N., land mines and unexploded ordinance killed or injured an average of two Iraqis every week. Landmines have also killed animals.

THE (FORMERLY) WET WORLD OF THE MARSH ARABS

Iraq's delta region was once a vast, lush wetlands. This is where the Tigris and the Euphrates rivers split into rivulets, streams, and lakes as they flow into the Persian Gulf. Some people think this valley is the location of the biblical Garden of Eden—or the inspiration for the mythical place—as described in both the Bible and the Qur'an. Some say it could be the site of the Great Flood, for which Noah built his ark, and the place where the patriarch Abraham was born. Whatever one's beliefs about these stories, be they history or allegory, it's clear that the Mesopotamian marshland region plays an important role in the religions of Judaism, Christianity, and Islam.

These marshlands have supported human communities and wildlife for 5,000 years. They are the ancestral home of Iraq's Marsh Arabs, or Ma'dan people, the cultural descendants of the ancient Sumerian and Babylonian civilizations. Until their world literally drained away, these people lived in much the same way as their ancient ancestors—raising water buffalo, sheep, and cattle, and fishing in the plentiful waters. The marshlands were also a wintering stop for migratory birds and a breeding spot for local animals, some of which have become extinct with the shrinking of their natural habitat.

Then Saddam Hussein's regime embarked on a series of large-scale hydro-engineering projects, with no regard for the environmental and human damage it would cause. More than thirty large dams were constructed over forty years. Massive drainage works in the 1990s were Saddam's retaliation against the Marsh Arabs for political insurrection. The marshlands shrunk from 7,700 square miles (20,000 square km) to less than 770 square miles (2,000 square km)—more than 90 percent—leaving behind cracked earth. Many scientists have described the situation as "one of the world's greatest environmental disasters."

It was also a human disaster, as the Ma'dan people suffered and scattered, leaving behind their old ways. After the fall of Saddam in 2003, the international community jumped in to help re-establish the historic marshes, but full restoration may not be possible.

In addition, Iraq suffers a severe shortage of doctors. Some 70 percent of physicians left the country after 2003 to escape the violence. Aid organizations such as Doctors Without Borders and Save the Children have brought volunteer professionals to help the remaining health professionals. As damage and health assessments reveal the effects of the wars on the Iraqi people, the most urgent efforts to repair and restore the environment include cleaning up oil-polluted areas, repairing water and sewage treatment facilities, and properly disposing of hazardous metals from detonated war weapons.

Medical staff wait for incoming patients at the emergency entrance of the al-Kadmiya Hospital in Baghdad.

INTERNET LINKS

newswatch.nationalgeographic.com/2013/04/29/8000-years-after-its-advent-agriculture-is-withering-in-southern-iraq
A National Geographic report on water shortages in Iraq and their effect on agriculture.

dai.com/stories/re-greening-iraq-restoring-marshlands
A report on one company's work since 2003 to restore Iraq's marshlands.

marshlands.unep.or.jp
Overview of the U.N. Environmental Programme's work for Iraq's marshlands.

www.natureiraq.org/"www.natureiraq.org
The site of a non-governmental organization committed to the protection of Iraq's environment.

IRAQIS

An Iraqi Kurd in the town of Halabja recalls the attack against Iraqi citizens by President Saddam Hussein in 1988. Up to 5,000 Kurds

MESOPOTAMIAN HISTORY COUNTS conquerors and immigrants as residents of the land between the rivers. Today more than three-quarters of Iraqis are Arabs, at least 15 percent are Kurds, and the rest include Turkomans, Persians, and Assyrians.

Young boys look after their cattle in the marshes of southern Iraq.

6

Years of war and unrelenting violence have left deep scars on a generation of Iraq's children. The Ministry of Labor and Social Affairs estimates some 4.5 million orphans live in the country–a country with only eighteen orphanages and fewer than two hundred social workers and psychiatrists put together.

Among the Iraqis, there are tensions between certain ethic groups and religious factions. Iraq has a large Kurdish minority in the north, for example, many of whom would prefer to form their own independent state. The rift between Sunni and Shia Muslims appears to be deepening, and members of minority religions complain of discrimination.

Some Bedouin people still roam the desert with their camels and livestock, but few of these traditional Arab nomads remain in Iraq.

THE ARABS

Iraq is part of the Arab world, which stretches from Iraq and Syria downward to Sudan and Somalia, and from Oman and the United Arab Emirates westward to Morocco and Mauritania in northern Africa. Most Iraqis are Arabs who speak Arabic and follow the Islamic faith.

HISTORY OF THE PEOPLE The Arab people originated in the Arabian Peninsula, which was separated from the rest of the ancient world by the sea on three sides and by the Euphrates River and the great desert in the north. The ancient Arabs lived in small clans consisting of several families. The clans were constantly at war with one another and raided one another's villages. The Arabs were aggressive and considered it honorable to die in battle. Acts of vengeance for the death of clan members were common.

In the seventh century, the Arabs began converting to Islam. They helped Prophet Muhammad to spread Islam in the Middle East. In so doing, the Arabs settled in new lands, where they drove out nonbelievers. In a short span of time, the Arabs became the primary inhabitants of Iraq and other countries in the Middle East and northern Africa.

THE BEDOUIN The Bedouin are an Arab people that have recently begun making a transition from their traditional nomadic lifestyle to living as settled farmers. There are still nomadic Bedouin living out of portable tents in the

desert, roaming in search of grazing land for their livestock. In the 1860s Bedouin made up more than 30 percent of Iraq's population; today they are less than 1 percent.

MODERN ARABS Iraqi Arabs strongly believe in religion, tradition, and family. Families are close knit, and elders are highly respected. Traditionally, Arabs are very generous to strangers and very supportive of friends, with whom they form lasting bonds.

The growing economic disparity among Arab countries is a cause of conflict. Some, such as the tiny countries of Kuwait and the United Arab Emirates, have grown rich on oil exports. Others, such as Iraq, have not. Despite having the second-largest oil reserves in the world, most Iraqis are very poor because of dictatorship, war, and sanctions.

Economic disparities in the Arab world and within Arab countries have raised discontent over several issues among poorer Arabs. These issues include the lack of trade and joint ventures between Arab nations, the lavish spending by the richer states on ostentatious airports and palaces, and the plight of the Palestinians.

A view of Iraq's neighborhoods shows low, square housing units and high-rise apartment buildings.

THE KURDS

The Kurds live in the mountains of northern Iraq and are the largest non-Arab ethnic group in the country. The Iraqi Kurds are part of a larger Kurdish region that covers western Iran, northwestern Syria, eastern Turkey, and Armenia (of the former Soviet Union). The Kurds have European origins, and have a language and culture different from that of the Arabs. The Kurds hope to gain independence and form their own nation, Kurdistan.

Iraqi Kurds have fought for independence since the 1950s. Under the leadership of Mustafa Barzani, the Kurds gathered strength and posed a serious threat to the Arabs. They formed guerrilla groups and launched attacks on the central government in Baghdad. The attacks intensified during the Iraq-Iran War.

In 1988 Saddam Hussein retaliated. Iraqi troops flew over Kurdish regions and dumped poisonous gas on some settlements. In just one

A Kurdish woman in a village near the Iraq border with Turkey

offensive, more than 5,000 Kurds were killed. The situation worsened after the 1991 Gulf War. As Iraqi troops retreated from Kuwait, they moved north toward the Kurdish region to punish the Kurds for refusing to support Hussein. As the Kurds fled into the mountains and escaped to Turkey or Iran, the Republican Guard systematically destroyed Kurdish towns and villages.

Almost all Kurds are Sunni Muslims; the Faili and a few minor tribes are Shia Muslims. One small Kurdish group, the Yazidi, have an unusual, mystical religion that distinguishes them from other Kurds. Other Kurds distance themselves from the Yazidi because of their religion, and the Yazidi likewise keep themselves separate from other groups.

Kurdish Iraqis have a European heritage and govern their own semi-autonomous region in the north of Iraq.

OTHER MINORITIES

Apart from the Kurds, there are other, smaller minority groups in Iraq. These include the Turkomans, the Assyrians and Armenians, and the Persians. In addition to these groups, Iraq has recently seen an influx of refugees from the political crisis in its war-torn neighbor, Syria, many of whom are settling in refugee camps in Anbar Province. And growing numbers of Iraqi refugees are returning to Iraq from neighboring countries, including Syria.

The Turkomans make up around 3 percent of the Iraqi population. They speak a Turkish dialect and are Sunni Muslims. They live in villages around Mosul and Kirkuk in the northeast.

The Assyrians are descendants of the ancient Mesopotamians. They speak Aramaic and are Christians. They live in northeastern Iraq and belong to the middle- and upper-class social brackets. The Armenians live mainly in Baghdad and are also Christians. Many came as traders in the early seventeenth century during the Ottoman—Persian wars. The Persians of

Iraq live mainly in Karbala, An Najaf, and Samarra.

SOCIAL SYSTEM

Iraqi society generally consists of three main classes: upper, middle, and lower. A person's social status is usually determined by birth, but the class system does allow for a degree of upward mobility.

An Iraqi teacher instructs a class of girls.

UPPER CLASS Members of the Iraqi upper class include government officials, wealthy people with distinguished ancestors, and influential individuals. Wealth is not a guarantee of upper-class status. In addition to being rich, Iraqis must have a good family name or hold an important position to be considered upper-class citizens.

MIDDLE CLASS Teachers, military personnel, government employees, small landowners, and businesspeople are among those who make up the Iraqi middle class. They are usually college-educated, moderately wealthy, and live in cities.

More Iraqis moved up into the middle-class social bracket during the 1970s and the 1980s when the government made available more opportunities for education.

LOWER CLASS Iraq's lower class consists of farmers, rural workers, manual laborers, and the unemployed. Iraqis do not place a stigma on members of the lower class. Although this class does not mix with the upper class, there is very little tension between the groups.

DRESS

Generally, Iraqis in the cities dress Western-style, while rural Iraqis still dress in traditional Arab attire.

TRADITIONAL MENSWEAR   Men in Iraq traditionally wear the *thobe* (THOH-bay), an ankle-length caftan with long sleeves. In the past, men wore colorful caftans, but today these are plain. This roomy garment allows air to circulate inside, which helps to cool the body in the heat of the desert.

A light cotton caftan, usually white, is preferred during summer because it is cool. In winter men wear caftans of heavier fabric, such as wool, in darker shades of grey or black. Another gown may be worn over the thobe for added warmth.

One of the most distinguishing features of the traditional Iraqi man's attire is the headcloth, called a *kaffiyeh* (kah-fee-YEH) in central and northern Iraq, and a *gutra* (GOO-trah) in the south. The headcloth is a square piece of cloth that is folded to form a triangle. It is usually made from cotton or

Typical mens' headwear is seen on these Iraqis who are performing midday prayer.

An Iraqi tailor sews a decorative edging on a traditional abaya.

wool, and is commonly plain white or checkered red. Worn over a skull cap, the headcloth may be twisted around the top of the head like a turban, or draped over the head like a flowing veil. It is often held in place by an *igaal* (ee-GAAL), a twisted, black, rope-like coil that circles the top of the head like a wreath.

More than a decorative piece, the kaffiyeh, or gutra, has a practical use—it protects Iraqi men from the sun's rays and the night cold. Bedouin men who live in the open desert find the headcloth especially useful in sandstorms, as they can pull the cloth over the mouth and nose to keep out the fine airborne sand.

Kurdish men wear Western-style clothes most of the time. They wear their traditional clothes during special occasions such as weddings and festivals.

Traditional Kurdish menswear usually consists of a pair of baggy wide pants called *pantaloons*, secured by a cummerbund sash around the waist; a skull cap; and a fringed turban in red checks, blue, brown, or white.

In winter, Kurdish men wear woolen turbans, and they may wear one long-sleeved shirt over another, or a vest over a shirt.

TRADITIONAL WOMEN'S WEAR Iraqi women wear a dark-colored cloak called *abaya* (ah-BAH-yah) that covers the body from head to ankle except for the face. The plain, bulky abaya may appear like a uniform but for the individual's personal touches. For a start, the fabric used for each abaya varies in shade and texture.

In addition, younger women often decorate their cloaks with gold-colored embroidery or bright-colored fringes, while wealthier women belt their abaya with a wide, jeweled girdle. A dress is worn under the abaya.

Unlike in certain other Arab nations, in Iraq women are not required by law or custom to veil themselves in public, although they may if they choose to. Many of the modern, educated women in Iraq's cities have switched from traditional Arab to Western-style dress. But for women in Iraq's rural towns, the abaya is essential for modesty.

Many women in the rural areas also wear a face veil, a practice that began in the Middle East as far back as 1500 BCE. These women cannot accept the thought of leaving their arms, legs, or face exposed when they leave the house and are shocked by the boldness of urban women who go out in public without the safety of the abaya.

Traditional Kurdish women's wear consists of two layers, one long, bright-colored dress over another. In addition, Muslim Kurdish women wear a headscarf. Like Kurdish men, Kurdish women wear Western-style clothes, reserving their traditional clothes for special occasions.

A veiled Iraqi woman walks with veiled daughter in Baghdad in 2014.

INTERNET LINKS

web.mit.edu/humancostiraq
Iraq: The Human Cost
A report from the MIT Center for International Studies on the consequences of the U.S. invasion and war on the Iraq people.

www.ibtimes.com/25-years-after-worst-chemical-weaponmassacre-history-saddam-husseins-attack-halabja-iraq-city
International Business Times
A story about the aftermath of the gas attack on Halabja.

LIFESTYLE

A girl holds radishes at an outdoor market.

THE LIFESTYLE OF IRAQIS IS determined and molded by their basic values and beliefs. One of the most important values is family loyalty. The family is a cohesive social unit that nurtures its young and old alike. Iraqis also greatly value a person's honor and dignity, and take all efforts to maintain an honorable reputation. Central beliefs held by all Iraqis include the ultimate controlling nature of fate, differences between men and women, and the increase of wisdom with age.

Iraqis are generous and loyal people. They are very polite to friends, who are also expected to fulfill certain duties. If a friend asks a favor, it is considered very rude to turn him or her down. A stranger is not given the same consideration as a friend, which may cause Iraqis to appear rude to foreigners. Once personal contact is made, however, Iraqis change their manner and become very accommodating and pleasant. An invitation to a person's home is considered a great honor and must never be turned down.

7

Nepotism, the practice of hiring one's family and friends, is considered unfair favoritism in the United States. But in Iraq, it is the usual way of doing business. Iraqis believe it is sensible to hire people you trust.

FAMILY LIFE

The family is the most important social unit in Iraqi society. Iraqis consider it a disgrace to speak badly of family members or to talk to outsiders about family problems. An Iraqi family consists of all related kin, which can include hundreds of people. Most Iraqis feel a strong affiliation to their relatives and make conscious efforts to maintain close family ties. Iraqis cherish their children and place their family above everything else.

In a traditional Iraqi family, each member has a clearly defined role. Children are expected to respect and obey their parents and grandparents, while grandparents offer advice and depend on their children to take care of them. The mother traditionally serves as the loving and compassionate figure in the household. She is expected to care for both her children and her parents as well as look after the household, but she has limited influence in decisions. The father is traditionally recognized as the head of the family. He is the disciplinarian and figure of authority.

LINEAGE   Iraqis, especially those in the upper and middle classes, are proud of their ancestral lineage. A family high up the social ladder uses its status to secure high-paying jobs and attract influential friends. Lower-class Iraqis also take pride in their family name and try to prevent their family's reputation from being tarnished.

MARRIAGE

Most Iraqi marriages are arranged by the family. Several things are taken into account for marriage, such as the potential partner's character, background, and financial position. Once two families decide upon a marriage, the man and woman meet and become acquainted. If either is dissatisfied with the match, the marriage is cancelled. More and more young, educated Iraqis in the cities are choosing their own partners, although they still seek their parents' approval.

In rural areas, marriages between first or second cousins are fairly common, particularly among tribal communities. Such marriages barely

A young bride, seventeen, is led from her home by her husband on their wedding day in Baghdad.

exist in the cities. Tribes arrange marriages between relatives because they can confidently judge the background and character of the bride and groom and keep money and property within the family.

Until a few decades ago, when polygamy was outlawed in Iraq, men married more than one woman. Muslim men can have up to four wives at a time, but this is discouraged in Iraq, where men have to apply for permission in court to have more than one wife.

Marriages in Iraq are based on financial security and companionship. For unsuccessful marriages, divorce is permissible by Islamic law. Both men and women must obtain a divorce through court proceedings, although it is easier for a man to obtain a divorce.

An Iraqi man must pay his divorced wife enough money to support herself and her children. Both parties can remarry without any stigma attached to them. Children of divorced parents normally live with their mother until they are seven to nine years old. After age nine, they are allowed to choose with whom they want to live.

PROPER SOCIAL BEHAVIOR

Men's and women's roles in Iraqi society have changed in recent years. Women had been given more freedom than before, largely because of the eight-year war with Iran and the 1991 Gulf War. As men left their jobs to join the armed forces and fight in the wars, positions in law, medicine, and business were open to women for the first time. Iraqi law approved the status of professional women because there were not enough men to fill the vacant positions. However, a shift to more conservative attitudes in recent years might reverse this trend.

Although women have joined men in the labor force, there are still clearly defined social behaviors for each of the sexes. Men and women, even husbands and wives, are segregated in public. When friends get together, the sexes usually divide among themselves. It is considered improper for an unmarried man and an unmarried woman to be alone together. Even men and women who work together avoid sustained contact with the opposite sex. Traditional Iraqis prefer this norm of gender separation, finding that they feel more comfortable in social settings this way. Platonic friendships between a man and a woman are rarely heard of in Iraqi society.

In rural areas, men and women follow the traditional social norms. Women rarely leave the house except to visit friends. It is considered improper for a woman to be seen in public without her veil or to shop in the market. An unmarried woman's reputation is ruined if she is seen with a man.

Men and women in rural areas are completely segregated. Even married couples rarely spend time together except while sleeping and eating. Men work and spend their leisure time in the company of other men. Women spend their time raising children, cooking, weaving, and socializing with friends.

CHILDREN

Iraqi parents love and cherish their children, yet raise them with strict discipline. The young are taught from an early age the importance of honoring and respecting the elder members of society.

Unlike children in the United States, children in Iraq usually live with their parents until they marry. Often, young adults choose to continue living with their parents even after marriage. If a newly married couple moves out of their parents' home, their parents will help finance their new home.

Alongside lessons in love and security, discipline is inculcated at an early age. Bad behavior will not go unpunished, and the child is warned to never repeat the act. Parents tend not to reason with their children or try to rationalize their misbehavior.

Iraqi children grow up with their siblings and cousins. The adults in their life include parents, grandparents, aunts, and uncles. The cohesive nature of Iraqi families shows children the strength of the family unit.

EDUCATION

Iraq's education system has three levels: primary, secondary, and college.

Iraqi youth receive their elementary education between ages six and twelve and attend secondary school between ages twelve and eighteen. During the last three years of secondary school, students are allowed to

A small number of private schools, such as this girls' school, offer an alternative to the poorly funded public schools.

Iraqi medical students at the University of Basra College of Medicine listen to a lecture.

choose between college preparatory classes or vocational school. Students in vocational schools learn trade skills in agriculture, industry, home economics, and commerce.

Colleges and universities offer the highest level of education in Iraq. There are several public universities, including four in Baghdad and others in Basra, Mosul, Arbil, Tikrit, Al-Kufah, Al-Qadisiyah, and Al-Anbar.

The quality of education in Iraq improved dramatically after the 1958 revolution. Education was provided free by the government up to college level. Before 1991 Iraq had one of the best education systems in the region, with a 100-percent enrollment rate in primary schools and high levels of literacy among both men and women.

However, like so much else in Iraq, the educational system suffered from the years of war and sanctions. Thousands of schools were damaged, looted, and lacked basic facilities. Functioning schools are overcrowded and degenerated, lacking electricity, sanitation, and teaching equipment. Many children have dropped out of school to help support their family, and literacy rates have fallen, especially among women. Since 2003, international agencies have been working to rehabilitate Iraq's schools and recruit new teachers. However, rebuilding the country's education system and infrastructure remains a major priority and challenge for the new administration in Iraq.

CITY LIFE

In the past sixty years, there has been a widespread migration of Iraqis to urban centers. The Basra and Al-Qadisiyah regions recorded the greatest movement of rural population to cities. These waves of migration have had an interesting effect. Iraq's urbanites were once a collection of individuals who left home to start a new life. Today the cities are filled with neighborhoods of friends and relatives, and this has made the cities warmer and friendlier.

During an economic slump in the 1950s, Iraqis were forced to build mud homes and live in crowded shantytowns. The government began to subsidize housing projects to accommodate the growing population. During the gulf wars, many families left Baghdad for the countryside further north to escape allied bombing.

RURAL LIFE

Iraq's villages consist of families that make up a tribe. The village tribe is usually governed by a sheikh, who lives in the largest house. The tribe includes resident tradesmen and government officials. Villagers live in small houses made of mud bricks. Their customs are deeply rooted in tradition. In most households, elderly parents live with their eldest son and his family. Other family members live in nearby houses in the village.

Parents prefer to send their children to religious schools. Children follow in their parents' footsteps in choosing a career. For instance, the son of a blacksmith usually becomes a blacksmith. Since the villages' economic base is agriculture, most villages lie on the banks of the Tigris or Euphrates. Water from the rivers is pumped to the villages by primitive means to irrigate the farms. Agriculture and raising livestock are the main occupations of villagers.

INTERNET LINKS

english.alarabiya.net/en/life-style/art-and-culture/2013/10/22/ Dance-Diplomacy-Iraqi-break-dancers-share-message-with-U-S-audience.html
A fun article about a group of young breakdancers in Iraq.

www.thisamericanlife.org/radio-archives/episode/416/iraq-after-us?act=0
This American Life: "Iraq After Us" (2010)
This recording of the radio show is a fascinating story of postwar life in Iraq on human terms.

RELIGION

The spectacular Jalil Khayat Mosque in Erbil was completed in 2007. It was named for a wealthy local resident who funded it.

8

RELIGION IS ONE OF THE MOST important aspects of life in Iraq. Almost everyone in Iraq feels strongly about their faith. Those perceived as not leading a religious life are often shunned by their neighbors. Atheists and agnostics are not easily accepted.

An Iraqi Jewish prayer book. At this point, very few Jews, if any, remain in the country.

One of the world's oldest communities of Jews–dating back some 2,600 years–once lived peacefully in Iraq. In the 1930s, when Nazi ideology swept through Europe, Iraqi Jews began to experience discrimination. After Israel became a Jewish state in 1948, conditions for Jews in Iraq became life-threatening. Tens of thousands left Iraq in the following years.

Iraqis try to pray and practice their religion daily. Religion pervades many activities. It is taught in classrooms; it dictates marriage and divorce laws; and it often plays a part in business and banking.

About 97 percent of the people are Muslims; they are divided into two sects: *Shia* (SHEE-a) and *Sunni* (SOON-nee). Shia and Sunni Muslims differ in some of their practices. Shia Muslims make up 60—65 percent of the population, Sunni Muslims 32—37 percent.

ISLAM IS BORN

Mesopotamia had as many religions as there were ethnic groups. Each invasion and change of rule introduced a new religion to Mesopotamia.

In 588 or 587 BCE the Chaldean king Nebuchadnezzar II destroyed Jerusalem and exiled thousands of Jews in Babylon. Many Jews later fled from Mesopotamia to escape persecution when the Mesopotamians adopted the religious beliefs of the new conquerors.

Islam came to the region in 637 CE when the Arab Muslims defeated the Iranian Sassanids. The majority of the population became Muslims, including the Kurds. Mass arrivals of Arabs from Oman and eastern Arabia bolstered the Mesopotamian Muslim population. Small Christian and Jewish communities retained their faith and remained in Mesopotamia.

Until the coming of Islam, Mesopotamia was a collage of different religions. People worshiped the gods of their tribes and families. The teachings of Prophet Muhammad gathered the multi-religious people under one faith.

FROM ADAM TO MUHAMMAD

To understand Iraqi culture, it is important to look at Islam. Muslims believe that God, or Allah, created the world and the first man, Adam. Adam was the first person to worship Allah, and also the first prophet. Adam's descendant Ishmael went to Mecca, and Ishmael's descendants grew up in present-day Saudi Arabia.

After Adam, there were other prophets tasked with spreading and reinforcing Islam. Some of the more well-known prophets, according to

The hajj occurs in Zulhijjah, the last month of the Islamic lunar calendar, more exactly between 8 and 13 Zulhijjah. The pilgrims conduct rites such as the following:

• Wearing a white seamless garment. This symbolizes purity and the equality of every person in the eyes of God.

• Standing at the plain of Arafat. This reminds pilgrims of the Day of Judgment.

• Collecting small pebbles at Mudzalifah and throwing them at white pillars in Mina. This reenacts Abraham's efforts to chase away Satan, who tempted him to disobey God.

• Sacrificing a goat or sheep. This commemorates how God, in appreciation of Abraham's steadfastness, replaced Abraham's son with a sheep at the time of the sacrifice.

• Walking seven times around the Ka'bah, a cube-like monument built by Abraham that sits in the Grand Mosque.

• Kissing or touching the Black Stone in the Ka'bah. Prophet Muhammad kissed the stone when he made his pilgrimage. Muslims believe that the stone was light-colored and shining when the angel Gabriel brought it from heaven and that it became black with the sins of humankind.

• Running seven times between the Safa and Marwa hills. This recalls Hagar's frantic attempts to find water for her baby, Ishmael.

Islam, were Noah, Abraham, Moses, and Jesus.

Muslims believe that Muhammad was the last prophet and God's messenger. Muhammad was born in Mecca around 571 BCE, a time of unrest. There was a lot of fighting and killing. The kind and benevolent Muhammad removed himself from society, because he was saddened by all the evil. Muslims believe that during one of Muhammad's meditative retreats on a mountain, the angel Gabriel came to him with the first revelation from Allah.

Muhammad told his wife about his experience, and she became the first convert to Islam. Despite hostile opposition from religious leaders in Mecca, Muhammad converted thousands to Islam. When he died, almost the entire Arab world, including Iraq, had become Muslim.

Muslims believe that the Qur'an was dictated by God. It instructs on the four major concepts in Islam: God, Creation, Man, and Judgment Day. Muslims believe that the soul lives on after physical death in the splendor of heaven or in the suffering of hell.

FIVE PILLARS OF ISLAM

Islam is based on a set of strict principles called the Five Pillars of Islam.

CREED   The Islamic creed declares that "there is no God but Allah, and Muhammad is His prophet." This is the premise on which a Muslim's faith is built.

PRAYER   Muslims must pray five times a day, facing the Ka'bah in the holy city of Mecca in Saudi Arabia. Muslims gather for worship at the mosque, but they are free to pray anywhere.

Friday is set aside as the holy day, and at noon Muslims converge in the mosques for worship. As in many other Arab countries, in Iraq many businesses and stores close on Fridays in observance of this holy day of the week.

CHARITY   Every Muslim who has the means is expected to give money to the less fortunate every year at the end of the fast of Ramadan. One of the reasons for this is so that the poor and needy can join in the Eid al-Fitr celebration. In addition, wealthy Muslims are expected to give to charity whenever their possessions meet certain conditions. This is for the general good and prosperity of society, to prevent poverty. It also keeps selfishness and greed at bay.

FASTING During the month of Ramadan, Muslims fast and abstain from food, drink, and sex daily from dawn to dusk. They must also avoid futile activities such as lying or harming others. Fighting during the Iraq-Iran War stopped for the holy month of Ramadan.

Fasting helps Muslims understand the plight of the poor and hungry and to be more willing to extend a helping hand. It trains Muslims to be patient, disciplined, and compassionate, while removing base desires such as greed and an excessive love for material things. Fasting is also beneficial to health and weight management. Above all, Muslims fast to bring themselves closer to God.

Almost all Muslims fast during the month of Ramadan; exceptions are very young children, the sick, the old, and women who are pregnant, breastfeeding, or menstruating.

PILGRIMAGE Muslims are expected to make the pilgrimage, or *hajj*, to the holy city of Mecca at least once in their lives, if they can afford to. Every year, more than two million Muslims from countries all over the world gather in Mecca for the hajj. Muslims believe that a successful pilgrimage cleanses them from all their previous sins, making them as pure as newborns by the time they go back home.

CHRISTIANS AND JEWS

Christians make up the largest non-Muslim group in Iraq. Many Iraqi Christians are Assyrian Christians, or Nestorians. The Nestorians broke away from the Roman Catholic Church in the fifth century due to a doctrinal disagreement, and founded their own church. But the largest church in Iraq is the Chaldean Church, established in the sixteenth century when some Nestorians reunited with the Roman Catholic Church in doctrine but kept their Eastern rite practices in worship. Sunday is the universal Christian holy day, when all Christians attend church to worship God as a community. Sunday is a day of rest, when many Christian businesses and shops in Iraq's cities close.

Jews have lived in Iraq since Mesopotamian times. Throughout their

Among the major world religions, Islam, Christianity, and Judaism are most closely related. There are distinct differences among the three faiths, but also notable similarities.

Christianity and Judaism share the books of the Old Testament in the Christian Bible. Islam and Christianity share several beliefs, including the existence of both heaven and hell; the birth of Jesus Christ to a virgin, Mary; and Jesus' ability to perform miracles.

Both the Qur'an and the Bible describe the story of the creation of the human race in the first man and woman, Adam and Eve. Both holy books emphasize the importance of faith in God and talk about the Day of Judgment. Both faiths share prophets such as Adam, Noah, Abraham, and Moses.

However, a major difference between Islam and Christianity, perhaps the most significant difference, is the identity of Jesus. While Muslims believe that Jesus was a prophet, Christians believe that he was the son of God made flesh, God and man at the same time.

Nonetheless, Muslims believe that Islam belongs to the same root of faith as do Christianity and Judaism. Indeed, a close comparison of the Qur'an, the Bible, and the Tanakh (the Jewish Bible), reveal the common foundations on which the three faiths are built.

history, Iraqi Jews have suffered persecution and displacement. Mob attacks in the 1940s injured or killed many Jews in Iraq. In the years following the birth of the state of Israel in 1948, Operations Ezra and Nechemia saw more than 100,000 Jews leave Iraq for Israel. More Jews left Iraq after emigration restrictions were lifted in the early 1970s, and today there are very few Jews, and possibly even no Jews at all, left in Iraq.

RELIGIOUS LEGACY Several stories from the Bible have been linked to places in Iraq. Abraham, the patriarch of the Jews, was born in Ur, an ancient city in southern Iraq. The prophet Daniel was thrown into the furnace of Nebuchadnezzar's palace in Babylon and was unharmed because he was a believer of God. Many also believe that the Garden of Eden, where Adam and Eve lived before their fall into sin, is in a village called Al-Qurna, some forty-six miles (74 km) north of Basra where the Tigris and Euphrates rivers meet. Adam supposedly first spoke to God at a eucalyptus tree in Al-Qurna known as Adam's Tree.

St. Joseph Church, a Chaldean Christian church, in the Kurdistan region of Iraq, was finished in 1980. It was built in the style of a Babylonian ziggurat.

INTERNET LINKS

www.nytimes.com/2008/03/04/world/middleeast/04youth.html
"Violence Leaves Young Iraqis Doubting Clerics"
An inside look at the concerns of Iraqi teens in a time of violence and uncertainty.

www.religionfacts.com/islam/index.htm
Religion Facts: "Just the facts on religion" offers a full overview of Islam.

www.beautifulmosque.com/jalil-khayat-mosque-in-erbil-iraq
See amazing photos of the new Jalil-Khayat Mosque, including exquisite tile work on the interiors.

www.projetaladin.org/holocaust/en/muslims-and-jews/muslims-and-jews-in-history/history-of-the-jews-in-iraq.html
The Aladdin Project seeks to build understanding between Jews and Muslims.

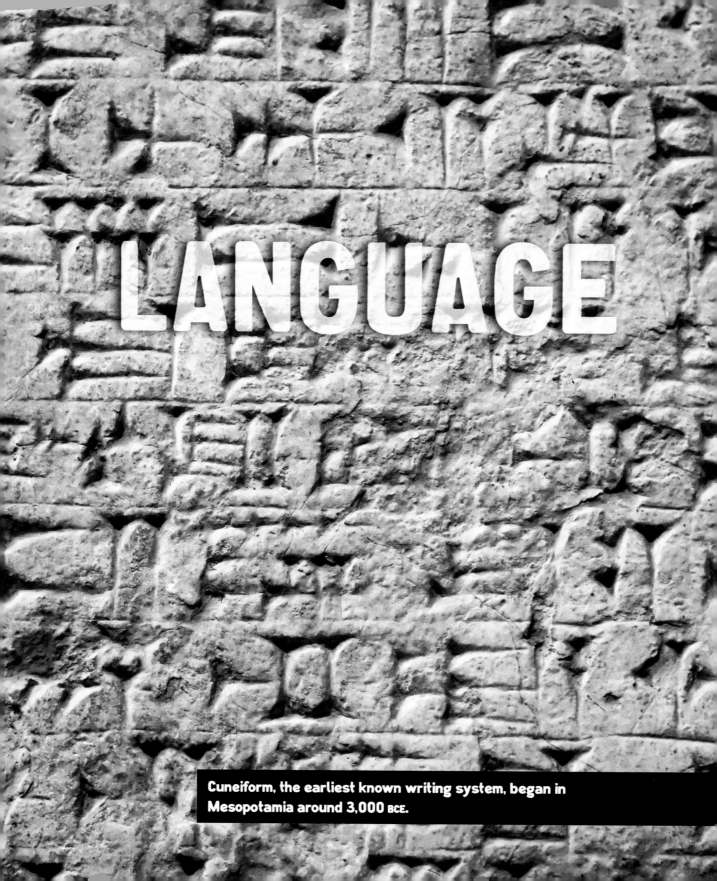

LANGUAGE

Cuneiform, the earliest known writing system, began in Mesopotamia around 3,000 BCE.

9

THE OFFICIAL LANGUAGE OF IRAQ is Arabic, which is also the official language of the Middle Eastern Arab nations and the language of Islam. Minority groups in Iraq speak some Arabic in addition to their mother tongue, such as Armenian, Kurdish, Syriac, or Turkish.

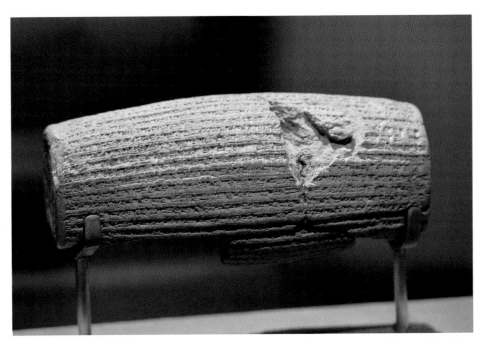

The Cyrus Cylinder, dating from 539 BCE, is an inscribed clay document describing the conquest of Babylon by Cyrus, the king of Persia, and how he saved the city from its evil former king Nabonidus.

Cuneiform started with pictographs and evolved over the centuries into wedge-shaped symbols. Eventually the symbols indicated spoken sounds rather than meanings. The symbols were adapted for use in various languages and changed into different alphabets.

Arabic is read from right to left, while English and other languages that use the Roman alphabet are read from left to right.

Kurdish is the largest minority language spoken in Iraq and is also spoken in Turkey, Iran, Syria, and Armenia. Kurdish is written in Roman, Arabic, and Cyrillic scripts. The Assyrians, who live mostly in northern Iraq, speak Syriac, which is a dialect of Aramaic, believed to be the language of Jesus Christ and his Apostles. The Turkomans speak a Turkish dialect that is related to languages spoken in Central Asia and Mongolia.

ARABIC

Arabic, one of the major languages of the world and the sixth official language of the United Nations, is the sacred language of Islam. Some 280 million people, or more than 4 percent of the world's population, speak it as their native language. Arabic is the fifth-most commonly spoken language in the world. It is a Semitic language, like Hebrew, and the roots of these languages go back thousands of years. Today Arabic has many variations that are used across North Africa, and the Middle East. Arabic originated in Saudi Arabia

BODY LANGUAGE

Nonverbal communication is an important part of interpersonal interaction in Iraq. Gestures and facial expressions may convey thoughts and feelings that are not expressed in words or may confirm the meaning of something that has been said.

Iraqis use their eyes and hands as they speak, to emphasize a point. In a conversation, Iraqis often stand closer to each other and touch each other on the arm more often than people from many Western cultures ordinarily do.

Traditionally, Iraqis also hold hands when talking to someone of the same sex, even if they are virtual strangers. Women generally do not use gestures as much as men do.

Iraqis greet people with a lot of enthusiasm. Members of the same sex kiss each other on the cheek or embrace each other. However, members of the opposite sex greet without physical contact. Even married couples traditionally avoid showing affection through gestures when they greet each other in public.

A few universal Arab gestures and their meanings include:

1. *When an Iraqi, or any Muslim for that matter, places his or her right hand over the heart after shaking hands with you, the person is expressing sincerity.*
2. *A raised fist with an extended thumb is a sign of victory.*
3. *Holding the right hand out, palm facing down, and moving it up and down means "be quiet."*
4. *Moving the forefinger of the right hand from right to left means "no" or "don't do that." Other signs that mean a negative response include raising the eyebrows and tilting the head back; and making clicking sounds with the tongue.*
5. *Holding the right hand out while opening and closing the palm means "come here"; moving the right hand, palm facing down, away from the body means "go away."*

before the fifth century BCE. Prophet Muhammad preached in Arabic, and the language quickly spread to the near East, Persia, Egypt, and northern Africa.

Arabic consists of three different tongues: classical Arabic, colloquial Arabic, and modern standard Arabic. Classical Arabic is used in the Qur'an. Colloquial Arabic varies from region to region. In Iraq the colloquial tongue is called Iraqi Arabic. Each area has its own version of spoken Arabic, and

Iraqis enjoy conversation in a coffee shop.

people from different regions often find it difficult to understand one another when they speak in their local tongues.

Modern standard Arabic is the official written form in Iraq and other Arab countries.

Arabic has an alphabet of twenty-nine letters—twenty-six consonants and three vowels. Arabic is written from right to left, and there is no difference between capital and small letters.

Some Arab words may not be as foreign as they sound to the native English ear. Due to the early Islamic conquests of various countries and centuries of trade between the Middle East and Europe, several Western languages, such as English, French, German, Italian, Portuguese, and Spanish, have adopted some Arabic words. Arabic words used in English include *arsenal*, *cotton*, *giraffe*, *lime*, *magazine*, *sofa*, and *sugar*.

CONVERSATIONS

It is not common in Iraq for a man and a woman who are not close acquaintances to converse with each other. Unlike in Western cultures, men and women in Iraq rarely interact in public places such as cafés, cinemas, or restaurants.

When Iraqis converse with their friends, it is customary for them to ask each other personal questions, about the other person's marriage, children, and salary, for example. While a Westerner might find such questions intrusive even among friends, an Iraqi would be offended by the reverse— not being asked such questions.

Iraqis also tend to repeat important information when conversing or to interrupt if they have something important to say; nor would they be offended by being interrupted. When more than two close friends get together, their conversation is likely to be loud and animated.

NAMES

Iraqi names are long; they include a first name, the father's name, the paternal grandfather's name, and the family name. People are addressed by their first name, which may be preceded by Mr., Mrs., Dr., or Miss. Parents are often politely addressed by their eldest son's name preceded by their parental title: *Umm* for the mother; *Abu* for the father. So the parents of a boy named Abdi would be called Umm Abdi and Abu Abdi.

After marriage, an Iraqi woman does not legally adopt her husband's name. Instead, she retains her mother's family name. Names often indicate not only a person's family but their religious affiliation and country of origin as well. Iraqis with Western names are Christians, while names beginning with *Abdel* or containing *deen* belong to Muslims.

Men often have the same first and third name because they are named after their paternal grandfather. An English equivalent of this pattern might be Thomas Samuel Thomas Jones. When an Iraqi's name becomes too long, a few parts of the person's name will be dropped. As a rule, his or her father's name and family name will be retained, but the others can be eliminated. Because of this practice, children of the same family often have different names or a different combination of names.

INTERNET LINKS

www.al-bab.com
Al-Bab: An Open Door to the Arab World (Click on Arab language).

www.arabic-language.org
This site features the Arabic alphabet, phrases, history, and more.

www.omniglot.com/writing/arabic.htm
Omniglot is an online encyclopedia of writing systems and languages.

video.pbs.org/video/1496198833
"The History of Writing" is an online video produced by PBS.

ARTS

Carpet weaving has a rich history in the Islamic arts.

10

RAQ HAS AN EXTENSIVE ARTISTIC history. The site of the first great civilization in the world, Iraq has produced inspiring literature, beautiful crafts and carpets, and grand architectural styles.

As archaeologists continue to excavate the ruins of ancient Mesopotamian cities, more exciting historical discoveries are being made each year. One famous Mesopotamian work of art is the Ishtar Gate, one of eight built by Nebuchadnezzar II. The gate is covered with blue glazed

A group of Iraqi art students paint concrete barriers that protect buildings from explosions.

"An archaeological site is a kind of a book. This book has to be read page by page. If you destroy these pages, you lose a tremendous amount of information. The southern part of the country is part of Sumer, the first civilization. They are destroying the beginning of mankind."
--Donny George, 2005, director of the National Museum of Iraq, refering to the looting of Iraq's archaeological sites

Tourists view a reconstruction of the original Ishtar Gate from ancient Babylon. The Gate is in a museum in Germany.

bricks and reliefs of bulls, dragons, and lions dedicated to Babylon's deities. The artwork on the gate was produced in fine detail. A reconstruction of the Ishtar Gate resides in the Pergamon Museum in Berlin, Germany.

ISLAMIC ART

Islamic art forbids the artist to portray any human or animal forms. That is why Islamic art depicts repeated patterns such as flowers or geometric designs. Many pieces of Islamic art contain Qur'anic inscriptions, and beautiful Arabic script adorns most of the pieces.

Islamic pottery is colorful and ornate. Materials used in the production of pots range from bronze to earthenware. Gold and silver were absent in ancient Islamic art, because these materials were strictly forbidden by Prophet Muhammad.

Carpets are some of the most magnificent artifacts in Islamic art. They are woven from fine threads in magnificent colors and are the object of many stories in Iraqi culture.

EARLY ISLAMIC ART When the Muslim conquerors overthrew the Sassanid dynasty in 637 CE, they inherited the state treasury. To increase their prestige, they used their newfound wealth to commission many works of art and architecture.

Wealthy Mesopotamians hired artists to weave beautiful carpets of special design for the family. In the middle of the eighth century, pottery and the textile industry became popular in the Islamic art circle. More wealthy citizens and the royal family hired talented artists to create innovative and elaborate designs. Their generous patronage of the arts encouraged artists to develop new modes of artistic expression. This inspired the great variety of Islamic art that people have appreciated for centuries.

Some of the commissioned artifacts included glass goblets or bowls decorated with elaborate designs in bright colors. Islamic glasswork ranged from bottles and drinking glasses to vases to flasks and pitchers, and from painted to colored to copper- or silver-stained. Islamic glass-makers used a variety of techniques that included gilding and enameling.

As a patron's art collection grew, he often commissioned the construction of a museum to house the valuable artifacts. The citizens of the community were invited to these museums to view the artworks on display. Generous patrons gave their private museums to their cities or to Muslim institutions, for the benefit of the entire community.

A detail of three warriors on the Ishtar Gate, from the time of King Nebuchadnezar II, 604-562 BCE

VISUAL ARTS

Television, film, painting, and sculpture are the main visual arts of modern Iraq. The popularity of television and film in Iraqi culture has greatly increased in recent years. After the war in 2003, a U.S. media operation replaced an

An art show
outside the
Baghdad Cultural
Centre attracts
viewers in 2013.

Iraqi television channel, providing local and world news via satellite. This new channel reported directly to the U.S. military.

Painting and sculpture are traditional Iraqi arts. Most paintings are housed in museums or homes in cities around the country. Under the Baathist regime, paintings and statues of Saddam Hussein appeared all over the nation. When Baghdad fell to U.S. forces in April 2003, some Iraqis celebrated the end of Hussein's regime by pulling down his statue. Others defaced images of him on murals and posters throughout the city.

LITERATURE

Early Iraqi literature originated as stories passed down from one generation to the next. These stories have contributed to Middle Eastern and Western literature throughout history. Stories, places, and books in the Bible, such as the Garden of Eden, the Psalms, and the Song of Solomon, have strong connections to Mesopotamian culture. Many Greek epic poems and myths, such as *The Iliad* and *Aesop's Fables*, are also based on Mesopotamian stories.

Iraq's most famous pieces of literature are the *Epic of Gilgamesh* and *A Thousand and One Nights*. The first is an Akkadian epic poem that tells

When Baghdad fell to U.S. forces in April 2003, the city erupted into chaos. Jubilant Iraqis took to the streets to celebrate the fall of Saddam Hussein. A sense of lawlessness quickly descended, however, and the scene become one of crazed destruction. Gangs of revelers demolished all symbols of the Hussein regime. They invaded government buildings and homes of government officials, stealing furniture, appliances, and supplies of all sorts. They looted stores and factories. However, things turned ugly, as they often do in such chaotic situations.

Mobs ransacked the National Museum of Iraq, the country's world class museum of art and antiquities. Looters stole priceless artifacts—many dating from the dawn of civilization—about 15,000 objects in all. The museum staff tried to protect the collections but were overrun and forced to abandon the building. The U.S. was sharply criticized for not protecting the museum.

Most looters were average, poorly educated citizens caught up in the frenzy of the moment. Many saw no difference between taking artwork and taking an air conditioner from a government office building. Both items belonged to the hated government, and ultimately, they reasoned, to the people. But some of the bandits were professional art thieves who had clearly been preparing for just this occasion. They knew the plan of the building, and went directly for the most treasured items, bypassing less valuable objects.

Most of the museum's 170,000 items were eventually found to be safe, having been locked away and hidden by the staff. And more than a quarter of the stolen objects have been recovered. Nevertheless, more than ten years after the looting, the museum is far from restored. It remains closed to the public, and opens only by appointment. The existing staff—those who did not flee the country— lack the expertise to evaluate, identify, and repair the artifacts. Despite the international community's desire to help revitalize the museum, ongoing violence in Iraq has kept away many experts from other countries.

of the adventures of Gilgamesh, the ruler of Erech, who tried to attain immortality. *A Thousand and One Nights* is a collection of thrilling stories of voyages, romance, and adventure. While much of Iraq's oral literature has been recorded and reproduced, Iraqis still enjoy literature through the art of storytelling.

Iraqi literature experienced a rebirth in the 1950s when, after centuries of cultural decay following the end of the Abbasid caliphate, many brilliant works were written. Besides the great increase in volume, the literature reflected a changing style. Epic stories were replaced by short stories that were filled with the everyday struggles and experiences of people in Iraq. Iraqi poetry styles also developed into the non-rhyming personalized form that was already popular in the Western world.

MUSIC

Traditional instruments used to make Iraqi music include the drums, fiddle, lute, oud, and violin. During Baghdad's days of glory, its music influenced

An Iraqi boy plays the oud in a school concert. The oud is a traditional Middle Eastern stringed instrument.

Arab-Islamic performance styles that spread as far as Spain. There are modern Iraqi musicians who have gained fame in the Arab world. They have to work abroad, because there is limited access to modern technology in Iraq due to wars and sanctions. Despite such restrictions, Iraq boasts a national symphony, opera house, and theaters that are packed during performances. Productions often depict the trauma and humor experienced by Iraqis in their daily struggles.

CRAFTS

Handicrafts are a popular art form in Iraq. The main handicrafts made by Iraqis are blankets, jewelry, leather, pottery, and rugs. In villages and small towns, women make handicrafts as a leisure and social activity. They gather with their children in the afternoon to make household items, such as colorful hand-woven rugs and blankets. Several households often share ownership of a pottery wheel that is used to make bowls, jugs, and ornamental objects.

An artisan constructs a clay baking stove.

The ruins of a temple from Nippur, one of the oldest of all Sumerian cities, sits high on a hill overlooking the site of the ancient city.

ARCHAEOLOGICAL DIGS

Iraq is an archeologist's treasure trove. The discovery of Mesopotamian ruins has allowed archaeologists, historians, and the people of Iraq to better understand the complex and rich culture of Mesopotamia. Less than 10 percent of Iraq's 25,000 historical sites have been excavated, which means great potential for further discovery and revelation.

NIPPUR   In 1990 archaeologists uncovered a temple in the ancient city of Nippur. The temple was dedicated to Gula, the Babylonian goddess of healing. This suggested that the temple must have been a hospital or healing center. Within the temple, archaeologists discovered ancient artifacts such as a bronze dog figurine with an inscription to Gula, and statues of people holding their stomach, throat, or back as if in physical pain. Archaeologists believe that the inhabitants of Nippur and the nearby cities came to the temple for medical treatment. Tablets and statues with inscriptions allow historians

REBUILDING BABYLON

Some 25,000 historic cities are thought to lie under the ground in Iraq, although less than 10 percent have been excavated. One of the most famous is the 4000-year-old city of Babylon, which reached the height of its splendor in the sixth and seventh centuries BCE. During the time of King Nebuchadnezzar II, Babylon was the largest city in the world, covering about 4 square miles (10 square km). Nebuchadnezzar II lived in a 700-room palace surrounded by the famous Hanging Gardens and a maze of canals. In the center of the ancient city stood the Great Ziggurat of Marduk, which was possibly the biblical Tower of Babel.

The ruins of Babylon straddle the Euphrates River, 55 miles (88.5 km) south of Baghdad. The city had a wide bridge connecting the two banks of the river. It was surrounded by a long thick wall and was guarded by the Ishtar Gate. The wall and the hanging gardens were two of the Seven Wonders of the Ancient World, as described by the Greeks centuries later.

The first serious excavations of Babylon were conducted in the nineteenth century and continued off and on until World War I in 1917. During this time the famed Ishtar Gate, one of the splendid entrances to the city, was dismantled and taken to Germany, where it remains. It is on view as part of a reconstruction in Berlin's Pergamon Museum. Meanwhile, at Babylon itself, a replica has been built in its place.

In 1983, Saddam Hussein began a massive rebuilding effort in Babylon, restoring some of the site, but mostly building cheap new construction in imitation of it, to create a tourist attraction. He built himself a modern palace right on top of some of the ruins and named it Saddam Hill. Like the ancient kings, he wrote his name on many of the bricks, with inscriptions such as: "This was built by Saddam, son of Nebuchadnezzar, to glorify Iraq." The project did more harm than good as original materials were destroyed or clumsily restored, archaeologists say.

In 2003, U.S. troops occupied the site, causing further damage to the archaeological record. Military vehicles crushed ancient pavements and soldiers pried mementos from the ruins. Today only 2 percent of the city has been excavated.

to study the ancient practice of medicine, the use of herbs and plants, and the roles of doctors and magicians.

MASHKAN-SHAPIR In early 1989 archaeologists discovered the ruins of Mashkan-Shapir between the Tigris and Euphrates rivers. Historians believe that Mashkan-Shapir was a major Mesopotamian city around 2000 BCE. It was destroyed around 1720 BCE. Mashkan-Shapir was surrounded by a thick wall with hidden gates. Clay tablets and cylinders bearing Sumerian cuneiform were left along the wall. Many of the tablets were dedicated to Nergal, the ancient Babylonian god of death.

The site of Uruk, thought to be the world's oldest, or first, city. Its walls were built some 4,700 years ago by the Sumerian King Gilgamesh.

Within the city walls, the remains of a cemetery, palace, and temple were found. The discovery of employees' recorded hours on the city's walls and clay tablets tells about the work ethic and lifestyle of the Mesopotamians. Elaborate canals, streets, and neighborhoods suggest that Mashkan-Shapir had an advanced government.

ARCHITECTURE

Architectural styles in Iraq vary from modern to quaint and majestic to plain. Many high-rise apartment complexes and business offices have been built in Baghdad. In contrast, Iraqi villages and small towns have simple, low buildings.

The architectural design of Iraqi Islamic shrines and their landscapes is amazingly beautiful. The shrines are covered with detailed mosaics in bright colors, and their high, arched entrances are supported by tall, strong pillars. Above the entrances are hundreds of mirrors arranged to reflect the sunlight. Around the shrines are courtyards enclosed by walls that are topped with exquisitely carved golden domes and minarets. Two of the most famous shrines in Iraq are at Karbala and Najaf.

The entrance to the Sanctuary Mosque Al Kadhimain, in Baghdad, exhibits the exquisite blue tile work, Arabic script, and pointed arches that are often seen in Islamic architecture.

INTERNET LINKS

www.iraqiembassy.us/page/art-and-culture
Embassy of the Republic of Iraq
A nice overview of arts, sports, culture, and museums.

www.metmuseum.org/toah/ht/?period=06&region=wam
Heilbrunn Timeline of Art History: "Iraq (Mesopotamia) 500—1000 A.D."
This excellent interactive timeline from the Metropolitan Museum of Art in New York connects historical events to works of art.

www.theiraqmuseum.com
National Museum of Iraq (The Iraq Museum)
Features videos and 3-D views of antiquities.

www.cnn.com/2013/04/04/world/meast/iraq-babylon-tourism/
This site has several videos and a photo gallery about the reconstruction of Babylon.

LEISURE

Boys jump into the Tigris River in Baghdad to cool off in the July heat.

11

RAQIS ENJOY A VARIETY OF LEISURE activities, depending on which part of the country they live in. People in the northern region take advantage of the steep mountains and cooler climate for outdoor leisure activities such as hiking and camping. People in the more watery regions around the Tigris and Euphrates rivers take to fishing and swimming in summer. People in the cities visit museums, bazaars, and shopping malls. However, one leisure pursuit unites all of Iraq's regions— the national favorite sport of soccer.

COMPANIONSHIP

Visiting friends and relatives is a popular leisure activity for Iraqis; most people set aside time every day or once a week for visits. Children and teenagers spend time together playing sports and games and watching television. Young adults catch up with friends and relatives at elegant restaurants and dancing establishments. Older Iraqis spend time talking with their peers. Regardless of the activity Iraqis choose, they place great importance in spending their free time with those they care about.

SINDBAD THE SAILOR'S SEVEN JOURNEYS

Stories from A Thousand and One Nights *(also called* The Arabian Nights*) have their roots in ancient and medieval Arabic, Persian, Indian, Egyptian, and Mesopotamian folklore. They have been translated into many languages and made into films. One of the most popular characters from the collection is Sindbad the Sailor, who makes seven journeys across land and sea, overcoming danger and disaster with wit and strength.*

Sindbad first leaves Baghdad in search of adventure and wealth. His ship lands on a beautiful island that resembles Paradise but turns out to be a sleeping fish. When the fish wakes up, all of the men except Sindbad escape on the ship. His crew presumes him dead, and Sindbad lives on an island with a king, until he is able to return to his home.

On his second journey, Sindbad is deserted on an island with giant birds, poisonous serpents, and magnificent diamonds. He escapes the perilous island with several large diamonds and becomes a wealthy man with the sale of the gems. On his third journey, Sindbad encounters vicious apes, an angry giant, an ogre, and a deadly serpent. Once again, he escapes unharmed, finds precious goods, and returns to Baghdad even wealthier.

And so it goes, with Sindbad venturing forth through four more journeys that bring him to strange places filled with fantastical creatures, dangers, and rewards. In the end, of course, Sindbad—like so many other mythic travelers—returns to Baghdad to stay, never going in search of adventure again.

STORYTELLING

Iraqis love to tell stories. They tell tales of fortune, luck, sorrow, and religious significance. The most popular story in Iraq is *A Thousand and One Nights*, which was first told in Mesopotamia during the reign of Caliph Harun al-Rashid, around 800 CE.

The story begins with a king, Shahryar, who develops a distrust and hatred for all women after he is shocked by his wife's infidelity. From then on, Shahryar marries a new woman every day and has her killed the next morning. He continues to do this for years, until Scheherazade, the daughter of his minister, offers to marry him in an attempt to stop the daily killing of innocent women.

On their first night together, before Shahryar goes to sleep, Scheherazade tells him an exciting story. But she stops just before the climax. Shahryar becomes so anxious to find out how the story ends that he does not kill Scheherazade. Every night, for many nights, Scheherazade tells the king a bedtime story but withholds the ending until the next morning. Eventually, the king grows to love her and does not have her killed. Her exciting tales of adventure, love, fortune, princes, kings, and queens are the stories that have come to be known as *A Thousand and One Nights*, or *The Arabian Nights' Entertainment*. One of Scheherazade's most well-known stories tells about the famous adventurer Sindbad.

SPORTS

Iraqi participation in sports has grown in recent decades, but political turmoil has made it difficult for many athletes to excel internationally. Iraqis' favorite sport is soccer, known to most of the world as football. (It is not American football.) There is also a growing interest in basketball, boating, boxing, and volleyball.

SOCCER The most popular sport in the world is also the favorite sport of the Iraqis. In 1986 Iraq qualified for the soccer world cup competition, which was held in Mexico. Iraq became the first country in soccer history to qualify by playing all its competitive games in venues outside its home country due to the Iraq-Iran War.

Iraq is a member of the Asian Football Confederation, which was founded in 1954. Iraq also takes part in the confederation's Asian Cup competition, which is staged every four years.

Soccer has been a welcome distraction from the turmoil of sanctions and wars in the last two decades. Soon after the war in 2003, Iraq's national team was reassembled and began training for the 2004 Olympics. Due to a lack of infrastructure in Iraq, the players trained in Dubai in the United Arab Emirates. Iraq's professional soccer players continue to perform, with the support of thousands of boisterous fans at matches between local clubs as well as at international games.

OTHER SPORTS Iraqis enjoy swimming and boating at Iraq's two major rivers and in the Persian Gulf. The warmer temperatures in the southern

Iraqi children play football (soccer) on a street closed to traffic.

regions allow Iraqis to enjoy water sports for most of the year. However, the destruction caused by the Iraq-Iran War and the Gulf Wars has curtailed many water-related leisure activities in southern Iraq.

BAZAARS AND MUSEUMS

Baghdad is famous for its bazaars. Although most cities and villages in the country have them, Baghdad's are the largest and have the widest selection.

Visiting a bazaar, one is surrounded by throngs of people searching for the best deal. The bazaars offer a sumptuous array of fruit, fresh meat, and exotic spices. They attract Iraqis from all socioeconomic groups, although

The huge Qaysari Bazaar at Erbil, in Kurdistan, is one of the world's oldest marketplaces.

An Iraqi man fishes in the waters of Shatt al-Arab in Basra.

the wealthy families usually send someone to shop for them. The prices of items at the bazaars are usually arrived at through a heated bargaining process between the buyer and the seller.

Browsing of a different kind takes place in the museums.

As the cradle of civilization, Iraq is the custodian of ancient artifacts that record human history from as early as 12,000 BCE Iraq's museums house some of the finest antique pieces of art, which include articles found at archaeological digs. Exquisite jewels, elaborate thrones, and fancy combs from the many caliphs, kings, and rulers of Iraq are displayed. Many of these ancient artifacts were damaged during the war in 2003, and many more were stolen by looters in the chaos after the war. The loss of these artifacts represented a permanent and immense cultural loss.

RURAL ACTIVITIES

Unlike the city dwellers of Iraq, residents of the small villages and towns scattered around the country live a relatively simple life steeped in tradition. Men and women in the rural areas generally keep to their own gender in their daily occupations, including leisure activities.

ACTIVITIES FOR MEN   Most rural towns are located along one of the twin rivers, where fish are abundant. Men spend a lot of time hunting and fishing with friends. This is not just a good way to socialize; it is also possible to provide the family with food from the day's hunt or fishing. Hunting and fishing trips are exciting, and young boys eagerly await the day when their father will take them on such an expedition.

The men are usually responsible for buying food at the markets and bazaars. On market days, groups of men spend the day together while leisurely shopping for food.

ACTIVITIES FOR WOMEN   Women in small villages and towns visit one another almost every day. While their husbands are away from home, working or relaxing with other men, the women gather to talk, cook, or make handicrafts.

The women also take care of and plan activities for those among their children who are not yet in school.

INTERNET LINKS

www.iraqinews.com
Iraqi News is a private English-language online newspaper that covers a range of Iraqi issues, including business, politics, security, social issues, culture, entertainment and sport.

www.sacred-texts.com/neu/burt1k1
The Arabian Nights' Entertainments
Full text of the stories from the 1850 translation by Sir Richard Burton, including "Sindbad the Sailor's Seven Voyages," "Aladdin: or The Wonderful Lamp," "Ali Baba and the Forty Thieves," and more.

www.storynory.com/category/fairy-tales/1001-nights
Storynory
Audio readings with text of some stories from *One Thousand and One Nights.*

www.iraqfc.webs.com
The official site of the Iraq National Football Team.

FESTIVALS

Shia Muslims take part in the Eid al-Adha prayers in Baghdad.

12

WITH EVERYTHING THAT THE Iraqi people have had to endure in recent times, life may seem uncertain and chaotic. Holidays and festivals give people a chance to gather together for prayer and reflection, feasting and merrymaking. These occasions give structure and a sense of continuity in confusing times.

New Year's Eve fireworks explode on January 1, 2014, over Shanidar Park in Erbil, in the Kurdish region of Iraq.

The government of Iraq declared Christmas as an official holiday for the first time in 2008. Nevertheless, the small minority of Iraqis who are Christians celebrate Christmas quietly and cautiously, as terrorist incidents aimed against them are not uncommon on Christmas.

Many festivals in Iraq celebrate secular events such as the nation's independence, but most have a religious significance. The dates of the Islamic festivals are determined by the Islamic lunar calendar rather than by the Gregorian calendar. Therefore, these special days may coincide with different Gregorian dates.

Friday is a holy day for Muslims. Most business offices and all government institutions close every Friday. The only businesses that remain open are those managed by non-Muslims.

MUHARRAM

The Islamic New Year is celebrated in the month of Muharram, the first month of the Islamic calendar year. Muharram is especially important to Shia Muslims.

During Muharram, Shia Muslims visit the shrine of Imam Hussein to honor the grandson of Prophet Muhammad. Shia Muslims believe that Al-Hussein ibn Ali, also called the Third Imam, was killed in battle in 680 CE. Hussein's story is recounted on the first nine nights of Muharram. As believers listen to the highly emotional story, many cry and shout, "Oh, Hussein! Oh, Hussein!"

Other events commemorate Hussein's death. The people reenact his daughter's marriage and his burial. One of the most intriguing events of Muharram is a street procession of Shia Muslim men beating themselves and one another with chains, belts, and sticks. They willingly undergo such physical pain to imitate the sufferings of Hussein.

THE TREE AT THE BOUNDARY During the first week of Muharram, Shia Muslims tell the story of the Tree at the Boundary. According to legend, on the first night of Muharram, an angel shakes a tree at the boundary of Paradise and Earth. Each leaf on the tree represents a living person. If a leaf falls while the angel shakes the tree, the person whose name appears on the leaf will die in the coming year. No one knows which leaves fall off the tree. But when someone dies, Shia Muslims believe that that person's name was inscribed on a leaf that fell off the Tree at the Boundary on the first evening of Muharram.

ASHURA The tenth day of Muharram is called Ashura. After the ceremonial reenactment of Hussein's death, Iraqi Muslim women begin preparations for a feast for the men and children. The whole village or family gathers at nightfall for a big feast. The day is also associated with the landing of Noah's Ark. The mourning surrounding the death of Hussein is replaced by festivities to celebrate the perpetuation of humankind.

Muslims, Christians, and Jews believe that Noah gathered two of every living creature in the world and built an ark to protect them from a great flood. When the flood came, it destroyed all the creatures of the earth except those inside the ark. Noah and his crew survived inside the ark for forty days, after which they landed on dry ground and began life anew. Iraqi Muslims celebrate the landing of Noah's Ark on Ashura.

A Shia Muslim pilgrim carries a picture of Imam Hussein as she and others walk the streets of Karbala. They are commemorating Arbaeen, a solemn occasion forty days after Ashura that was once outlawed under Saddam Hussein.

RAMADAN

The fourth pillar of Islam is the observance of Ramadan, the month when Muslims fast from sunrise to sunset. Fasting Muslims remind themselves of their dependence on God and his blessings and draw closer to him by saying more prayers, giving more money to charity, and reading the Qur'an more often. Fasting requires a lot of self-discipline, especially when there is an abundance of food. Fasting enables Muslims to develop compassion for those who do not have enough to eat. The time to break the fast is indicated by the sound of a cannon explosion, usually broadcast on the radio, which follows the evening call to prayer announced at sunset by the muezzin at the mosque.

At the end of Ramadan, everyone gives alms, and the wealthy usually invite the less fortunate into their homes to feast with them.

EID AL-FITR

Eid al-Fitr (eed ahl-FITTER) is one of the biggest holidays in the Islamic calendar. It marks the end of the fasting month of Ramadan. Muslims celebrate the three-day Eid al-Fitr by feasting. Many people stay home during Eid al-Fitr and invite friends and relatives over to feast.

MAWLID AN-NABI

MAWLID AN-NABI (MAW-lid ahn-NEH-bee) celebrates the birthday of Prophet Muhammad. On this holiday, older Muslims relate the series of events that accompanied the birth of the prophet.

Angels descended upon the earth to assist in Prophet Muhammad's delivery. He was born with a light that lit up the space between the East and the West. The light illuminated the palaces of Syria, Lebanon, Palestine, and Jordan. Gazing into his face, Prophet Muhammad's mother saw that he shone like the moon and smelled of the finest perfume.

On the night that he was born, the earth shook until the pagan idols in Mecca collapsed and the fire in a Persian temple that had been worshiped for a thousand years was extinguished.

EID AL-ADHA

Eid al-Adha (eed ahl-AHD-ha) occurs in Zulhijjah, the twelfth month of the Islamic year, when Muslims visit Mecca, in Saudi Arabia, for the hajj. Every year on Eid al-Adha, Muslims celebrate the patriarch Abraham's love for God by visiting the graves of their relatives and giving food to the poor. The story of Abraham's faith goes like this: To test Abraham's loyalty, God told him to sacrifice his son Ishmael. Abraham told Ishmael about this command, and Ishmael asked his father to do it. As Abraham tearfully raised his knife, a miracle happened, and in Ishmael's place was a sheep instead. Abraham proved his faith in God, and God spared Ishmael.

Shiites pray together during Eid al-Adha, the Feast of the Sacrifice.

FAMILY CELEBRATIONS

WEDDINGS   The most exciting nonreligious celebrations in Iraq are weddings. Wedding festivities start a few days before the marriage ceremony, as relatives, friends, and acquaintances host parties to honor the couple.

On the day of the wedding, the bride and groom marry in a small ceremony, with only their relatives and closest friends present. After the ceremony, the wedding party parades through the streets, with residents cheering them to the newlyweds' home, where the bride and groom consummate their marriage.

The party continues to celebrate while waiting for the young couple. When the newlyweds emerge from their home, the party proceeds to a reception, and the celebration often lasts until the early morning hours.

BIRTHS Three days after the birth of a baby, friends and family visit the parents and the baby, usually bringing gifts for the child.

FESTIVALS AND HOLIDAYS IN IRAQ

The dates of the Islamic festivals are stated according to the Islamic calendar, which, like the Gregorian calendar, has twelve months. But the same festivals fall on different Gregorian dates, because the Islamic month, and thus the Islamic year, is slightly shorter.

Islamic Festivals

1 Muharram . . . .   *The Tree at the Boundary*

10 Muharram . . .   *Ashura*

12 Rabiul Awal . .   *Mawlid an-Nabi (Prophet Muhammad's birthday)*

Ramadan. . . . . . .   *Ramadan fast*

1 Syawal. . . . . . .   *Eid al-Fitr*

10 Zulhijjah. . . . .   *Eid al-Adha*

National Holidays

January 1. . . . . . .   *New Year's Day*

January 6. . . . . . .   *Army Day*

July 17 . . . .   *Anniversary of the Revolution*

October 3. . . . . . .   *Independence from British mandate*

Christian Festivals

April. . . . .   *Easter (exact date varies)*

December 25 . . . .   *Christmas*

The birth of a boy in Iraq is celebrated more than the birth of a girl. With the birth of each male child, superstitious rites are performed to provide protection throughout the boy's life. Foreign visitors and women without children are discouraged from attending the birth festivities, as this is considered bad luck.

AL' KHATMA The religious festival that Iraqi Muslims take most pride in is a child's reading of the Qur'an. Children diligently study the Qur'an for a year or more in preparation for al' Khatma, so that they can read the Qur'an without making any mistakes.

The reading of the Qur'an is a very difficult task. Children go through many sessions, boys reading to men and girls to women, until they complete the entire holy book. This requires a great deal of discipline and dedication, and the child's success is seen as a major accomplishment. Muslims believe that the reading of the Qur'an is the first step in receiving God's blessings and that the true sign of a gift from God is a person's ability to fully understand the meaning of Islam's holy book.

The al' Khatma ceremony is a very solemn occasion. The child receives the undivided attention of his or her peers and elders while reading. When a boy has read the Qur'an without error, he earns the title *hafiz* (HAH-fizz), while a girl who reads the Qur'an perfectly is called *hafizah* (HAH-fi-ZAH).

After the child has successfully read the Qur'an, the ceremony becomes a festival in his or her honor. The men usually hold a lunch for the boy, while the women celebrate with an afternoon tea for the girl. Friends and relatives of the hafiz or hafizah attend the festival and shower gifts and money on the honorary guest. All the attendants dress in colorful clothes and spend the afternoon celebrating the child's accomplishment.

INTERNET LINKS

hawlergov.org/en/index.php
The official site of the Erbil Governate in Kurdisan. Erbil has a famous festival, bazaar, and several parks.

www.natureiraq.org/green-festivals.htmlNature
Iraq sponsors the annual Green Music and Arts Festivals celebrating nature and conservation in Iraq.

www.reelfestivals.org
Reel Festivals sponsors Reel Iraq, a festival of Iraqi film, music, and literature.

FOOD

Baklava and other sweet pastries are on display in Mosul, a city in northern Iraq.

13

THE FLAVORS OF IRAQ ARE Mediterranean, Turkish, Greek, Persian, and of course Arab. They are the spicy flavors of cardamom, cinnamon, turmeric, and saffron; the fragrance of rosewater; the sweetness of dates; the earthiness of eggplant, chickpeas, and bulgur wheat; and the savory tastes of grilled onions and skewered meats.

A favorite Iraqi food is *ma'mounia*, a sweet semolina dessert that dates to the ninth century. A caliph requested a sumputous dish worthy of a king. His cook came up with a soft pudding garnished with almonds and cinnamon. It's still a popular dessert to this day.

A spice merchant prepares his fragrant goods for shoppers.

The staples in the Iraqi diet are wheat, barley, and rice. Women in small villages use wheat to make bread; barley is a main ingredient in many Iraqi dishes; and rice may be eaten as a main or side dish.

MEAT

The most important livestock in Iraq are sheep and goats, raised by nomadic and semi-nomadic groups for meat, milk, wool, and skins. In small villages, butchers slaughter a sheep or goat every day. Villagers hurry to the butcher to claim choice cuts for their dinner. Those who go to the butcher later in the day will find only the remains of a carcass. Iraqis cook almost every part of a sheep or goat. Delicacies include the kidneys, liver, and brain. The meat is usually cut into small strips and cooked with onions and garlic for flavor. Iraqis also enjoy mincing the meat for a stew that is served with rice. Other meats enjoyed in Iraq are fish, beef, chicken, and camel.

Since 1990 most Iraqis have survived on monthly rations of chicken, flour, sugar, and yeast. This has had a harmful effect on the health of the average Iraqi, particularly children aged one to five, as their daily diet lacks many essential vitamins and nutrients.

Islam forbids the consumption of pork, but Christians in Iraq have access to pork from Christian butchers.

MEALS DURING THE FASTING MONTH

During Ramadan, Muslims have their main meals before dawn and at sunset. Before dawn, Iraqis have a simple meal of fried egg or omelet with onions, and radish and broad beans. The meal is completed with dates and other fruit, a large glass of juice, and plenty of water.

After sundown, Iraqis break the fast with a light meal of dates, a yogurt drink or a thick apricot juice, and a bowl of soup. They have the second main meal half an hour later. This includes a lamb, beef, or chicken stew with rice, a vegetable dish, grilled or oven-baked fish, a salad, and bread.

TABLE MANNERS AND SOCIAL ETIQUETTE

The Iraqis have very strict rules concerning table manners. Here are some things to do or to avoid when dining with Iraqis:

- It is offensive to use one's left hand when eating. For traditional reasons, the left hand is considered unclean.
- It is considered proper for only one person to pay the bill in a restaurant. Iraqis are embarrassed by the Western custom of splitting the bill.
- Iraqis prepare a lot of food for parties or feasts. To be polite, the guests try to eat everything in front of them.
- It is not considered rude in Iraq to eat food quickly or without utensils. In fact, it is a sign to the host or hostess that the food is delicious.
- Iraqis are extremely offended if the family pet comes near the table during the meal.
- After eating, Iraqis lavishly praise the meal and the preparation of the food.
- When attending a meal prepared by someone else, an Iraqi will invariably bring a small gift to the host as a gesture of gratitude.

There are other rules that are as important as proper table manners in everyday life. The following are some general rules of Iraqi etiquette:

- Iraqis shake hands when greeting. When a man and a woman greet, the woman extends her hand first to indicate that she wants to shake hands.
- It is considered very rude to turn one's foot outward when talking to someone. Iraqis will be extremely offended if a person turns the sole of his or her foot toward them.
- If an Iraqi gives someone a gift, it should be accepted with both hands and opened in the absence of the benefactor.
- Iraqi men stand when a woman enters the room, and open doors for women. Both men and women stand when an older person enters or leaves the room.
- If someone admires an Iraqi's possession, such as a vase or small sculpture, the Iraqi will usually insist that the person take it. Therefore, it is proper etiquette to refrain from lavishly praising another's possessions.

FEASTING

Iraqis express their joy in and gratitude to God by holding feasts. Two important feasts take place during the Islamic year. One commemorates the end of Ramadan; the other celebrates the pilgrimage to Mecca.

A feast to an Iraqi is a celebration equivalent to a party. No one is left out of the celebration—neighbors, relatives, and friends are invited to partake in the festivities. Iraqi families spend hours preparing the food for the feast, and there is usually singing, dancing, and storytelling to go with the eating.

FAVORITE FOODS

A true Iraqi meal lives up to the word feast. There may be several appetizers, soups, salads, main courses, and desserts—with so many choices, an Iraqi meal often resembles a buffet.

A vendor grills fish on the street in Baghdad; he is preparing Iraq's national dish, *masgoof.*

A favorite Iraqi feast begins with salad and soup served with bread. Iraqi bread, *khubiz* (khoo-biz), is traditionally baked in a clay furnace and can make a filling meal when served with appetizers. Iraqi soups range from a thick lentil soup to a creamy chicken soup. Popular Iraqi salads include a mixture of pickled vegetables and a mixture of mashed potatoes with crushed wheat.

The main courses are simple but delicious and are often served with a tomato-based sauce mixed with okra. Kebabs, marinated lamb or chicken cubes skewered over a charcoal grill, are an all time favorite.

Fish from the Tigris is barbequed on bricks to make *masgoof* (mahs-GOOF). Other preferred dishes include roasted chicken or stewed lamb with rice.

DRINKS AND DESSERTS

The two most popular drinks among Iraqis are coffee and tea. Both are usually served either before or after a meal, rather than with food. Iraqis generally like their coffee sweet, with fresh cream or milk. Iraqis have an unusual tradition in the preparation of coffee. They will heat and cool the coffee nine times before serving, believing that this removes impurities. This practice is common in the smaller villages and towns, while urbanites prefer their coffee fast.

One common attribute of coffee drinking in Iraq is that it is a social activity. Iraqis like to have their coffee with family and friends at cafés, restaurants, parties, or at home.

During the summer months, most people enjoy a cool, refreshing glass of water. Soft drinks have become a luxury for most Iraqis. Although Islam forbids the consumption of alcohol, Iraq produces a very potent spirit, known as arak, from dates. Before the 1991 Gulf War, Iraq brewed its own beer and the northern regions produced wine. But the average Iraqi today cannot afford the luxury of alcohol.

Like many other Middle Easterners, the Iraqis are renowned for their desserts. Their favorites include an assortment of pastries with creamy fillings such as ground almonds or mashed dates, thin pancakes buried in layers of fruit and syrup, and a rich semolina and cinnamon pudding called ma'mounia.

Strong Arabic coffee is often served in small cups.

THE EID AL-FITR FEAST

Iraqis traditionally celebrate the end of Ramadan with a feast on Eid al-Fitr. In a village of approximately 300 people, one or two cows and five to seven grown sheep might be slaughtered. The internal organs of the animals would be prepared in a special way, and the rest of the meat roasted over a charcoal fire, cut into small pieces, and served with vegetables and rice.

The people of the village gather in one large room to share the meal.

A man picks up groceries for his household at an open-air market.

The men sit on one side of the room or move to another room altogether to have their meal apart from the women.

In the cities, the wealthy may have servants prepare and serve the feast. In more modest households, it is traditionally the women who are responsible for preparing and serving the food.

Wars and sanctions have greatly toned down Eid al-Fitr festivities in Iraq. For most Iraqis, feasting is a thing of the past, until their country recovers from its wounds, under a hopefully more democratic regime.

FOOD SHOPPING

The cities and villages of Iraq are filled with small food markets, which often form part of a larger group of markets called a bazaar, which sells a wide range of products from food to handicrafts.

The most successful food markets in Iraq sell fruit, vegetables, spices, or fresh meat. In the small villages and towns, the men do the marketing after deciding with their wives what the household needs.

Due to wars and sanctions, many Iraqis lost the means to buy food for their basic meals. They had to survive on food rations given out by Saddam Hussein's government. After the war in 2003, humanitarian aid organizations played a big part in alleviating the shortage of food that caused malnutrition and death, especially among children. (However, the crisis is by no means over.)

REGIONAL FOODS

Topography and weather play a major role in determining the favorite foods of a particular region. These factors traditionally restrict Iraqis' choice of fresh foods to those that are available to them in their region. Modern transportation, however, has widened the choice.

THE TIGRIS AND EUPHRATES RIVERS The residents of the areas surrounding the two main rivers of Iraq are blessed with a daily selection of fresh fish. Another favorite in the region is milk from the *jamoosa* (jah-MOO-sah), or water buffalo. The jamoosa's milk is rich and is used to make yogurt and butter. The yogurt is prepared by cooling the fresh milk overnight, scraping off the top layer, and adding a yogurt starter. Within hours, the yogurt is ready for eating, cooking, or diluting with water for a delicious drink.

THE NORTHERN REGION Iraqis of the northern regions, including the Kurds, eat meat from cows or chickens. Cows receive more nourishment in the cooler north and live healthier lives. Thus, the meat and milk from these cows is delicious and rich. The women of the northern regions prepare homemade tomato paste from homegrown tomatoes. Another regional delicacy is goat's milk, which is used to make white, preserved cheese.

Eggplant is a favorite vegetable throughout the Middle East, where it can be combined with meat, as in the following recipe, or stand on its own as a vegetarian main dish.

INTERNET LINKS

nawalcooking.blogspot.com
In My Iraqi Kitchen: Recipes, History and Culture, by Nawal Nasrallah
A cooking blog by the author of *Delights from the Garden of Eden: A Cookbook and a History of the Iraqi Cuisine.*

www.al-monitor.com/pulse/culture/2014/03/arab-coffee-culture-politics-society.html#
Learn about Arab coffee culture.

MEAT AND VEGETABLE CASSEROLE (*TEPSI BAYTINIJAN*)

1 large eggplant, peeled

2 teaspoons salt

½ cup oil

3 medium potatoes, peeled, cut
  into ½ inch thick round slices

2 medium onions, cut into ½ inch
  thick round slices

1 lb ground lamb or beef

4 garlic cloves, crushed

1 teaspoon pepper

1 teaspoon cumin powder

⅛ teaspoon cayenne

3 medium tomatoes, cut into ½ inch thick round slices

½ cup water

Preheat oven to 350°F. Halve the eggplant lengthwise, and slice it into half rounds about an inch thick. Sprinkle with 1/2 teaspoon salt. In a frying pan, heat oil over medium heat. Fry the eggplant slices on medium flame for six minutes or until lightly golden. Add more oil as necessary. Drain cooked slices on paper towels. In the same oil, lightly fry the potatoes and onions for five minutes. Set aside.

In a bowl, combine the meat, half the garlic, 1/2 teaspoon salt, 1/2 teaspoon pepper, and 1/2 teaspoons cumin and cayenne. Form into small balls. Fry the meatballs over medium heat for about 10 minutes, or until browned. Drain on paper towels.

Combine the water and remaining seasonings. Stir well and set aside.

Arrange slices of eggplant on the bottom of an oiled casserole dish. Place potato rounds on top, followed by tomatoes. Spread meatballs evenly between the tomato slices. Pour the seasoned water mixture on top. Cover and bake in a 350°F preheated oven for one hour. Serve warm.

IRAQ DATE COOKIES (*KLAYCHA AT-TAMR*)

2 cups flour
1 tsp. baking powder
1 tsp. ground cardamom
½ tsp. salt
¾ cup butter, melted
1 cup sugar
3 eggs, beaten
1 cup chopped dates
1 cup chopped walnuts

Sift together flour, baking powder, cardamom, and salt; set aside.

Thoroughly combine butter, sugar, and eggs; then gradually stir in dry ingredients until a soft dough is formed, adding a little water if necessary. Stir in dates and walnuts; then place heaping teaspoons of the dough an inch apart on an ungreased baking sheet. Place in an oven preheated to 350°F and bake for 15 minutes or until cookies turn golden brown. Remove and allow to cool before serving. Makes 45 cookies.

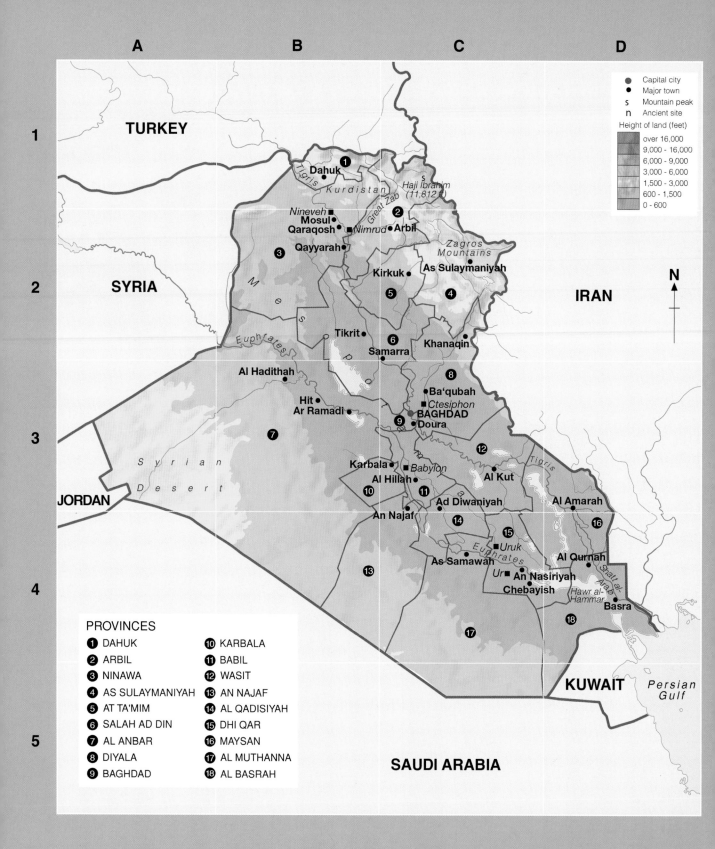

TURKEY

1

Dahuk ●
①

Tigris

Kurdistan

S
Haji Ibrahim
_(11,812 ft)_

SYRIA

Nineveh ■
Mosul ●
Qaraqosh ● ■ _Nimrud_
② ● **Arbil**

Great Zab

Qayyarah ●
③

_M_
_e_
_s_
_o_

Kirkuk ●
As Sulaymaniyah ●

Zagros
Mountains

2

IRAN

⑤
④

Euphrates

Tikrit ●
⑥

Khanaqin ●

Samarra

⑧

Al Hadithah ●

Ba'qubah ●
■ _Ctesiphon_

Hit ●
Ar Ramadi ●

⑨ ● **BAGHDAD**
● **Doura**

3

⑦

Syrian

Desert

Karbala ●
■ _Babylon_
Al Hillah ●

⑫

Al Kut ●

Tigris

JORDAN

⑩
⑪

Ad Diwaniyah ●
Al Amarah ●

An Najaf ●
⑭

⑯

⑬

⑮

Euphrates

Uruk ■
As Samawah ●

Al Qurnah ●

Ur ■ **An Nasiriyah** ●
Chebayish ●

Hawr al-
Hammar

Shatt al- Arab

Basra ●

⑰

⑱

KUWAIT

Persian
Gulf

SAUDI ARABIA

N

Legend:
● Capital city
● Major town
S Mountain peak
n Ancient site

Height of land (feet)
over 16,000
9,000 - 16,000
6,000 - 9,000
3,000 - 6,000
1,500 - 3,000
600 - 1,500
0 - 600

PROVINCES

① DAHUK
② ARBIL
③ NINAWA
④ AS SULAYMANIYAH
⑤ AT TA'MIM
⑥ SALAH AD DIN
⑦ AL ANBAR
⑧ DIYALA
⑨ BAGHDAD

⑩ KARBALA
⑪ BABIL
⑫ WASIT
⑬ AN NAJAF
⑭ AL QADISIYAH
⑮ DHI QAR
⑯ MAYSAN
⑰ AL MUTHANNA
⑱ AL BASRAH

Ad Diwaniyah, C3
Al Amarah, D3
Al Anbar (province),
 A3, A4, B3, B4, C3
Al Basrah
 (province), C4,
 D4, D5
Al Hadithah, B3
Al Hillah, C3
Al Kut, C3
Al Muthanna (pro-
 vince), C4—C5
An Najaf, C3
An Najaf (province),
 B3, B4, C3, C4
An Nasiriyah, C4
Al Qadisiyah (pro-
 vince), C3—C4
Al Qurnah, D4
Ar Ramadi, B3
Arbil, C2
Arbil (province),
 B1, B2, C1, C2
As Samawah, C4
As Sulaymaniyah,
 C2
As Sulaymaniyah
 (province), C1—
 C2
At Ta'mim
 (province), C2

Ba'qubah, C3
Babil (province),
 B3, C3
Babylon, C3
Baghdad, C3
Basra, D4

Chebayish, C4
Ctesiphon, C3

Dahuk, B1
Dahuk (province),
 B1
Dhi Qar (province),
 C3, C4, D4
Diyala (province),
 C2—C3
Doura, C3

Euphrates, A1, A2,
 B2, B3, C3, C4

Great Zab, B2, C1

Haji Ibrahim, C1
Hawr al-Hammar,
 D4
Hit, B3

Iran, C1—C3, D1—
 D4

Jordan, A3—A4

Karbala, C3
Karbala (province),
 B3—C3
Khanaqin, C2
Kirkuk, C2
Kurdistan, B1, B2,
 C1
Kuwait, D4—D5

Maysan (province),
 C3, C4, D3, D4
Mosul, B2

Nimrud, B2
Ninawa (province),
 B1—B2
Nineveh, B2

Persian Gulf, D4—
 D5

Salah ad Din (pro-
 vince), B2, B3,
 C2, C3
Samarra, C2
Shatt al-Arab, D4
Saudi Arabia, A3—
 A5, B4—B5, C4—
 C5, D5
Syria, A1—A3, B1—
 B2
Syrian Desert, A3—
 A4, B3—B4

Tigris, A1, B1—B3,
 C1—C3, D3—D4

Tikrit, B2
Turkey, A1, B1, C1

Ur, C4
Uruk, C4

Wasit (province),
 C3—C4

Qaraqosh, B2
Qayyarah, B2

Zagros Mountains,
 C2

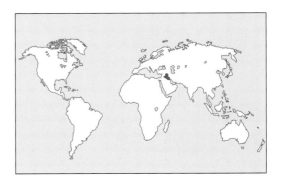

ECONOMIC IRAQ

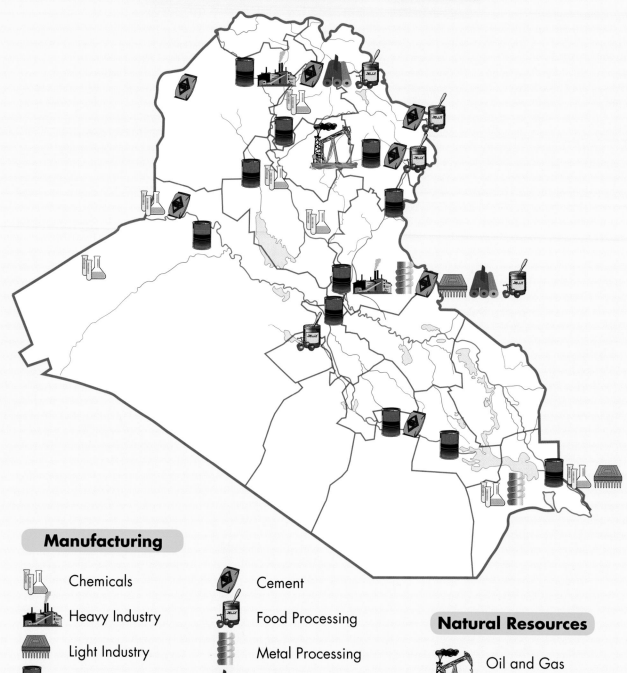

Manufacturing

Chemicals

Heavy Industry

Light Industry

Petroleum Refining

Cement

Food Processing

Metal Processing

Textiles

Natural Resources

Oil and Gas

ABOUT THE ECONOMY

OVERVIEW

A spike in violence during 2013–2014 slowed economic growth that had seen improvement since the end of the war. Broader economic development, long-term fiscal health, and sustained improvements in the overall standard of living still depend on the central government passing major policy reforms. Iraq's largely state-run economy is dominated by the oil sector. The government of Iraq is eager to attract additional foreign direct investment, but it faces a number of obstacles including a shaky political system and concerns about security and social stability. Rampant corruption, outdated infrastructure, insufficient essential services (such as electricity), skilled labor shortages, and outdated commercial laws stifle investment and continue to constrain growth of private, non-oil sectors.

CURRENCY

Inflation rendered coins, known as fils, obsolete; coins stopped being minted in 1990
Notes: 50, 250, 500, 1,000, 5,000, 10,000, 25,000 dinar
1 U.S. dollar (USD) = 1,166 Iraqi dinar (IQD) (2014)

INFLATION RATE

2 percent (2013)

GROSS DOMESTIC PRODUCT (GDP)

$248 billion (2013 est.)
Growth rate: 3.7 percent

AGRICULTURAL PRODUCTS

wheat, barley, rice, vegetables, dates, cotton, cattle, sheep, poultry

INDUSTRIAL PRODUCTS

petroleum, chemicals, textiles, leather, construction materials, food processing, fertilizer, metal fabrication/processing

LABOR FORCE

8.9 million (2010)

MAJOR EXPORTS

Crude oil

MAIN IMPORTS

Food, medicine, manufactured goods

TRADE PARTNERS

United States, India, Italy, France, Spain, Australia, China, Russia, Canada, South Korea, Turkey, Syria

EXTERNAL DEBT

$59.49 billion (2013 est.)

PORTS AND HARBORS

Basra, Khawr az Zubayr, Mina Al Bakr, Umm Qasr

OIL PRODUCTION CAPACITY

2.987 million bbl/day (2012 est.)

CULTURAL IRAQ

Al Hadba Minaret
Built in 1172 CE, this mosque in Mosul is famed for its 170-foot (52-m) bent minaret in elaborate brickwork.

Hatra
This ancient fortified city built under the influence of the Parthian Empire was also the capital of the first Arab kingdom.

Iraqi Museum
Looting after the 2003 war damaged and depleted one of the world's most important archaeological collections—more than 10,000 items from Mesopotamia and other ancient civilizations—in this museum in Baghdad.

Abbasid Palace
This thirteenth-century palace holds the echoes of the glorious Abbasid era, when Baghdad was the center of Arab Islamic civilization.

Nineveh
This rich archaeological site in Mosul was the capital of the Assyrian Empire.

Erbil
This ancient city once ruled by the Romans is said to be the oldest continuously inhabited city in the world.

Ctesiphon
The ruins of the capital of the Parthian and Persian empires demonstrate the splendor of Sassanian architecture.

Babylon
This great city was once ruled by Nebuchadnezzar II, who built the famous Hanging Gardens and the Ishtar Gate. This is also the site of the Tower of Babel.

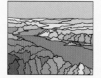

Tigris River
It was here that Islam and the Assyrian and Babylonian empires rose. The Tigris—with its twin, the Euphrates—provides a livelihood to the people of Iraq, Syria, and Turkey.

Ur
Established around 2100 BCE, Ur was the capital of the Sumerians, one of the first known civilizations that adopted a code of conduct and law for its people.

ABOUT THE CULTURE

OFFICIAL NAME
Republic of Iraq

NATIONAL FLAG
Adopted in 2008, three equal horizontal bands of red, white, and black. The phrase Allahu Akbar, meaning "God is great," is in green, Kufic script in the center of the white band.

NATIONAL ANTHEM
"Mawtini" ("My Homeland") (temporary anthem since 2004)
www.nationalanthems.info/iq.htm

CAPITAL
Baghdad

OTHER MAJOR CITIES
Basra, Mosul, Kirkuk

POPULATION
31,858,481 (2013 est.)

LIFE EXPECTANCY
Total population: 71.1 years
Male: 69.7 years
Female: 72.7 years (2013 est.)

ETHNIC GROUPS
Arab 75—80 percent, Kurdish 15—20 percent, Turkoman, Assyrian, or other 1 percent

RELIGIOUS GROUPS
Muslim 97 percent
Shia Muslim 60—65 percent; Sunni Muslim 32—37 percent; Christian or other 3 percent

LANGUAGES
Arabic (official); Armenian, Kurdish, Persian, Turkish (minority)

LITERACY RATE
total population: 78.5 percent
male: 86 percent
female: 71.2 percent (2011 est.)

ISLAMIC HOLIDAYS
The Tree at the Boundary (Muharram 1), Ashura (Muharram 10), Maulid an-Nabi (Rabiul Awal 12), Eid al-Fitr (Syawal 1), Eid al-Adha (Zulhijjah 10)

NATIONAL HOLIDAYS
New Year's Day (January 1), Army Day (January 6), Anniversary of the Revolution (July 17), Independence from British mandate (October 3)

POLITICAL LEADERS
Jalal Talabani—president (since 2005)
Nuri al-Maliki—prime minister (since 2006)

TIMELINE

IN IRAQ	IN THE WORLD
9000 BCE Settlers cultivate wild wheat and barley, domesticate dogs and sheep.	
3500 BCE Sumerians start the world's first known civilization, on the banks of the Euphrates.	
1900 BCE Babylonians conquer Mesopotamia.	
605 BCE Nebuchadnezzar II builds the Hanging Gardens and the Ishtar Gate.	**753 BCE** Rome is founded.
331 BCE Alexander the Great conquers Mesopotamia.	**116–17 BCE** The Roman Empire reaches its greatest extent, under Emperor Trajan (98–117).
637 CE Muslims invade Mesopotamia and convert its people to Islam.	**600 CE** Height of Mayan civilization
1258 Mongols attack; Islamic caliphate ends.	**1000** The Chinese perfect gunpowder and begin to use it in warfare.
1534 Turks seize Mesopotamia and annex it to the Ottoman Empire.	**1530** Beginning of trans-Atlantic slave trade organized by the Portuguese in Africa
	1558–1603 Reign of Elizabeth I of England
	1620 Pilgrims sail the Mayflower to America.
	1776 U.S. Declaration of Independence
	1789–99 French Revolution
1840 First archaeological excavation	**1861** U.S. Civil War begins.
	1869 The Suez Canal is opened.

IN IRAQ	IN THE WORLD
1917 British capture Baghdad from the Turks.	**1914** World War I begins.
1932 Iraq becomes an independent state.	**1939** World War II begins.
	1945 The United States drops atomic bombs on Hiroshima and Nagasaki.
	1949 North Atlantic Treaty Organization (NATO) is formed.
1958 General Abdul Karim Kassem leads a revolution that ends the monarchy.	**1957** Russians launch Sputnik.
1968 The Baath Party takes over the government.	**1966–69** Chinese Cultural Revolution
1979 Saddam Hussein becomes president.	
1980 Iraq-Iran war begins.	
1990 Iraq invades Kuwait.	**1986** Nuclear power disaster at Chernobyl in Ukraine
1991 Gulf War drives Iraqi forces out of Kuwait.	**1991** Break-up of the Soviet Union
1995 United Nations allows Iraq to export oil to buy food and medicine.	**1997** Hong Kong is returned to China.
	2001 Terrorists crash planes in New York, Washington, D.C., and Pennsylvania.
2003 U.S.-led strike ousts Saddam Hussein.	
2011 December—U.S. completes troop pull-out.	**2011** Tsunami hits Japan, causing more than 15,000 casualties
2014 Parliamentary elections set for April.	**2013** Argentine cleric Jorge Bergoglio becomes Pope Francis I, head of the Roman Catholic Church.

GLOSSARY

abaya (ah-BAH-yah)
A long dark-colored cloak worn by women that covers them from head to ankle.

cuneiform
The oldest known writing system in the world, used extensively in Mesopotamia and Persia. The characters have a wedge-shaped appearance.

Eid al-Adha (eed ahl-AHD-ha)
The Islamic festival celebrated in remembrance of Abraham's near-sacrifice of his son Ishmael and God's sparing of Ishmael's life in recognition of Abraham's faith.

Eid al-Fitr (eed ahl-FITTER)
The Islamic festival celebrated to end the month-long fast of Ramadan.

hajj
The pilgrimage to Mecca, required of all Muslims who are able to go.

Ka'bah (kah-AH-bah)
The holiest Islamic shrine in the world, situated in Mecca, Saudi Arabia.

Mesopotamia
Ancient Iraq; the region between the two main rivers of Iraq, the Tigris and the Euphrates.

muezzin
A man who calls Muslims to prayer from a mosque, via loudspeakers.

Muharram (MOO-hah-rahm)
The Islamic New Year and the first month of the Islamic calendar.

Qur'an
The holy book of Islam. Muslims believe that it was dictated by God to Prophet Muhammad.

Ramadan (rah-mah-DHAN)
The ninth month of the Islamic calendar, a time of fasting and atonement for sins.

sheikh
The leader of a village or tribe.

Shia
The majority Islamic sect in Iraq that recognizes Prophet Muhammad's son-in-law, Ali, as his heir.

Sunni
The minority Islamic sect in Iraq that recognizes another of Prophet Muhammad's relatives as his heir.

surah
A chapter in the Qur'an.

thobe (THOH-bay)
A long, loose, plain caftan with long sleeves that is traditionally worn by men.

ziggurat (ZIG-goo-raht)
An ancient Mesopotamian temple tower shaped like a pyramid with many storeys.

FOR FURTHER INFORMATION

BOOKS

Anonymous. *IraqiGirl: Diary of a Teenage Girl in Iraq*. Chicago: Haymarket Books, 2009.

Dalley, Stephanie. *Myths from Mesopotamia: Creation, the Flood, Gilgamesh, and Others*. New York: Oxford University Press, USA, 2009.

Myers, Walter Dean. *Sunrise Over Fallujah*. New York: Scholastic, 2008

Nasrallah, Nawal. *Delights from the Garden of Eden: A Cookbook and History of the Iraqi Cuisine*. Sheffield, England: Equinox Publishing, 2013.

Polk, William. *Understanding Iraq*. New York: HarperCollins Publishers, 2005.

Shadid, Anthony. *Night Draws Near*. New York: Picador, 2005.

Smithson, Ryan. *Ghosts of War: The True Story of a 19-Year-Old GI*. New York: HarperCollins Publishers, 2009.

Steele, Philip. *Mesopotamia (Eyewitness)*. New York: DK Publishing, 2007.

DVDS/FILMS

Iraq in Fragments. Seattle: Typecast Releasing, 2007.

The Iraq War. History Channel. New York: A&E Home Video, 2008.

My Country, My Country. New York: Zeitgeist Films, 2007.

Nature: Braving Iraq; Restoring the Garden of Eden. PBS, 2010.

WEBSITES

Central Intelligence Agency World Factbook (select Iraq from the country list). www.cia.gov/cia/publications/factbook

Embassy of the United States, Baghdad, Iraq. iraq.usembassy.gov

Iraq Daily (newspaper). www.iraqdaily.com

"Iraq (Mesopotamia) 500—1000 A.D.". In Heilbrunn Timeline of Art History. New York: The Metropolitan Museum of Art, 2000—. www.metmuseum.org/toah/ht/?period=06®ion=wam (October 2001)

Iraqi Cultural Office, Washington, DC iraqiculture-usa.com/geography

Library of Congress: Federal Research Division: Country Studies. memory.loc.gov/frd/cs/iqtoc.html

PBS Frontline. Iraq: Decade. www.pbs.org/wgbh/pages/frontline/iraq-decade

University of Chicago: Oriental Institute: Archeological Site Photography: Mesopotamia. oi.uchicago.edu/research/lab/photos/meso

BIBLIOGRAPHY

BOOKS

Bratman, Fred. *War in the Persian Gulf*. Brookfield: Millbrook Press, 1991.

Childs, N. *The Gulf War*. Vero Beach: Rourke, 1991.

Foster, Leila M. *Iraq*. Chicago: Childrens Press, 1990.

Iraq in Pictures. Visual Geography Series. Minneapolis: Lerner Publications Company, 1990.

Salzman, Marian and Ann O'Reilly. *War and Peace in the Persian Gulf: What Teenagers Want to Know*. Princeton: Peterson's Guides, 1991.

Tripp, Charles. *A History of Iraq*. Cambridge: University Press, 2000.

WEBSITES

Ancient History Encylopedia. www.ancient.eu.com/

Council on Foreign Relations. "Iraq's Faltering Infrastructure." 2006 www.cfr.org/iraq/iraqs-faltering-infrastructure/p10971

Iraq Business News. www.iraq-businessnews.com/tag/infrastructure/

INDEX

INDEX